# *Soul Maps*

# Soul Maps

## A Guide to the Mid-life Spirit

### Mardi Tindal

UNITED CHURCH
PUBLISHING HOUSE
Toronto, Canada

ANGLICAN
BOOK CENTRE
Toronto, Canada

Canadian Cataloguing in Publication Data

Tindal, Mardi
        Soul maps : a guide to the mid-life spirit

Includes bibliographical references.
ISBN 1-55134-115-8

1. Midlife crisis — Religious aspects — Christianity. I. Title.

BV4509.5.T56 2000          248.8'4          C00-930634-X

United Church Publishing House          Anglican Book Centre
3250 Bloor Street West, Suite 300        600 Jarvis Street
Etobicoke ON                             Toronto ON
Canada  M8X 2Y4                          Canada  M4Y 2J6
416-231-5931                             416-924-9192
bookpub@uccan.org                        abcpublishing@national.anglican.ca
www.uccan.org/ucph                       www.abcpublishing.com

Design, Editorial, and Production: Publishing, and Graphics and Print Units

Printed in Canada
5  4  3  2          04  03  02  01  00

990391

# Dedication

To Margaret and Norman,
Chris and Alex who grace my mid-life
from before and after, and

To Doug, my beloved partner who gracefully
travels beside me through the
mid-life adventure

# Contents

Preface / ix

Acknowledgements / xiii

Introduction / 3

Chapter 1: *Net Worth* / 7

Chapter 2: *Letting Go* / 29

Chapter 3: *The Personals* / 49

Chapter 4: *Cold Wars and Crumbling Walls* / 67

Chapter 5: *Getting It Together* / 83

Chapter 6: *Return on Investment* / 101

Conclusion: *Abundant Life—Playing on the Slide* / 115

Notes / 127

Resources Consulted / 128

Credits / 129

# *Preface*

*I* wrote this book because I needed to read it. At forty-six I was knee-deep in spiritual confusion as a person for whom spirit is critically important. I needed some mid-life wisdom so I went looking for wise, spiritually attuned mid-lifers and found them everywhere. They came from a variety of faith traditions, some from no faith tradition. Together they represented all kinds of life experience. And they told me that *they* needed to read the book too! So these pages represent collected wisdom from those for whom the spiritual dimension of life is as important as air, spun together in response to my own questions and my own mid-life reflections.

I had better tell you right away that this book does not pretend to provide a clear route through mid-life. Joan Didion is right when she says that it is impossible to ever get to the point of seeing a clearly marked open road to the years ahead. Consequently there can never be one singular guide to the mid-life spiritual journey. But as companions we are able to be guides to one another according to where we have found spiritual truth and nourishment on the mid-life path.

I also want you to know that this is not a scholarly sourcebook on mid-life psychology. Such books have already been written and I am indebted to experts who have pointed to major developmental markers on the journey. I have included a resource list to help you find at least some of them.

In addition to what I have learned from such writings, I wanted to hear from ordinary folks who take their souls as seriously as their psyches. I was curious about how mid-life faith evolves and grows—whether we are religiously involved or not. The people who told me their mid-life stories—Christian, Baha'i, Hindu, Jew, Muslim, Sikh, and those of no particular faith tradition—are people who take the spiritual dimension seriously, who know that when you have plumbed the depths of psychology, you have not come anywhere near the end of the human spirit.

Mid-life seekers generously gave me their time and insights, including their own strategies for surviving and thriving through mid-life muck. Whenever I explained that I was examining the mid-life soul, the first responses typically were about crisis. But, as conversations unfolded, mid-life joy was clearly mixed in with the anxiety. I offer here what I have learned through struggling with mid-life questions with these others as guides and companions.

My own introduction to focused thinking about mid-life came in the form of an invitation from a mid-life friend. Tim Scorer of Naramata Centre (a United Church Education and Retreat Centre in British Columbia) asked if I would work with him to develop and lead a ten-day retreat in response to the expressed need of parents of young adults. For decades Naramata has offered young adults what it calls Winter Session to help them sort out directions for their first life journey. Providing a corresponding program for mid-lifers was new for the centre and the concept was also new to me. My first reaction was to say "But I want to come as a participant!" Leading turned out to be a good way to participate and I am deeply grateful to Tim for the ongoing invitations to work with him on these week-long mid-life retreats. I also enjoy my work with Five Oaks Centre in Ontario where I am able to lead and coordinate mid-life retreats and other adult programs devoted to spiritual development at various life stages.

You will see in what follows that I wrote this book as a Christian with a broad sense of how every part of life is enhanced by paying attention to the spiritual—the invisible yet powerful currents that flow through and flow beyond daily experiences to give them ultimate meaning. The life and teachings of Jesus are for me the most compelling evidence of God's loving intentions for and involvement in the world. I have been profoundly shaped by my upbringing and participation in The United Church of Canada and as a result have a deep respect for and interest in what I can learn from those within and beyond my own faith tradition.

My hope is that this book is accessible and nourishing to a broad spectrum of mid-lifers, whether or not they have a lively connection with a religious community. I hope that if you are involved in a community of faith you will find not only fresh insight here for yourself but also an opportunity to explore these questions with others in your community.

One of the ways in which we affirm our faith in my church is to declare that "We are not alone—we live in God's world!"* My prayer is that the stories and reflections that you find here will help you to discover that you are not alone and that your mid-life spiritual crisis and joy is a precious part of God's creative world.

* from the Creed of The United Church of Canada

# Acknowledgments

*I* feel surrounded in mid-life—not only by current teachers and friends but by all of those who have helped me get this far. Countless people have offered their wisdom and provided the encouragement that has resulted in this book. I thank you all and acknowledge a few here.

First to my husband Doug whose deep friendship is a constant source of inspiration and support and who also happens to be an excellent editor. To my children, Chris and Alex who give me reasons to smile, reflect more deeply, and keep learning every day. All three of these men with whom I share a home have enabled me to do this writing.

To friends and colleagues including Tim Scorer at Naramata Centre who invited me to work with him to design a mid-life retreat several years ago and with whom I continue to lead these retreats, and to Yvonne Stewart and my other colleagues at Five Oaks Centre who have supported me in offering the same kind of programming at Five Oaks.

To John Bird whose sensitive letter when my father died appears in these pages.

I am especially indebted to all of those friends and acquaintances who allowed me to grill them about their experiences of mid-life including those with whom I conducted 'formal' interviews: Nina Acharya, Tony Badaloo, Angelos Bacopoulos, Fredelle Brief, Debbie Cantrell, Sherry Connolly, Hugh Drouin, Munir El-Kassem, Al Evans, Gerald Filson, Margaret Fisher Brillinger, John Green, Guru Raj Kaur Khalsa, Flora Litt, Paul Logan, Sybilla Mannsfeldt, Lynn McCabe, Marilyn Melville, Beth Parker, Esta Pomotov, Sheldon Reisler, Judy Robinson, Susan Scott, Ralph Singh, Judy Symington and 'Mary.' Their insights form the backbone of this book.

I also want to acknowledge a generous grant from the F.K. Morrow

Foundation that supported the publication of this book.

   Finally and with great gratitude I want to acknowledge both the encouragement and the professional expertise of the fine people at the United Church Publishing House.

# *Introduction*

> **"…we never reach a point at which our lives lie before us as a clearly marked open road, never have and never should expect a map to the years ahead."**
>
> *Joan Didion*, After Henry

*I* have been interested in developmental stages for a long time. When I was a twenty-two-year-old graduate student, I figured I knew all about the stages of moral and faith development. I had read and studied a bit with Lawrence Kohlberg at Harvard, was steeped in Jim Fowler's writing on faith development, and was learning from my thesis advisor, Ed Sullivan at the Ontario Institute for Studies in Education. But knowing the theories did not prepare me for immersion into my own mid-life crisis and joy.

My bookshelves sag from ever increasing volumes with titles like *Awakening at Mid-life* and *Mid-Life Directions* (see the Resources Consulted on page 128). There are slight variations in the ways in which writers define "mid-life" but most contend that its first glimmers are at about thirty-five years of age and that it continues to about sixty-five. One seventy-eight-year-old who talked with me contends that he is still in mid-life (though he concedes he may have to move on soon). He makes the point that shifting demographics have affected our definitions of life stages. If you are caring for parents in their nineties, he says, you are still in the middle.

Many have been informed by Carl Jung's writings about mid-life. Flora Litt is one of them. Flora provides spiritual companioning, helping people to listen to God themselves and to reflect upon how God has been and is with them on their life journey. One of the things she told me was that there is an internal imprint—a kind of pre-set program of human nature that determines that mid-life will be a time of deep questioning.

Writers like Anne Brennan and Janice Brewi, authors of *Mid-Life Directions* and other books about mid-life, describe how Jung presented the second half of life, beginning with mid-life, as being profoundly different from the first half of life, of childhood and youth. Similarly, I have chosen to speak here about the first and second journeys of life since the people I interviewed frequently spoke about how their lives in the middle were so different from when they were young.

The guidebook you hold in your hands is really a kind of scrapbook for the mid-life traveller. It provides others' accounts of where the road has taken them and what they have discovered on the way. It also gives you the opportunity to add your own accounts and reflections along the side trails of your own mid-life journey.

In addition to being a resource for personal use I invite you to use it to explore your spiritual journey with other mid-life travellers. Each chapter is a blend of my own discoveries combined with the discoveries of those with whom I talked and learned and seasoned with related questions for you to think about and discuss with others.

The first chapter, Net Worth, explores mid-life themes of meaning, worth, and work. The second chapter, Letting Go, is a compilation of the many things that mid-lifers told me they've had to let go of in order to continue growing spiritually. The Personals (chapter three) comes from my conversations about mid-life relationships with friends and with partners. Cold Wars and Crumbling Walls (chapter four) explores mid-life relationships with the generations on either side of us. Chapter five, Getting it Together, is about the relationship between mid-life physical and spiritual changes. Return on Investment (chapter six) presents a variety of views on how we can turn our middle lives outward to be a blessing to the world. Finally, chapter seven, Abundant Life, provides conclusions and tips for practising joyful mid-life spiritual development.

If you are using this book within a study group I recommend that you focus on one chapter each time you meet. Ideally you will be able to commit yourselves to a six-to-eight week process of regular discussions. Participants should read the relevant chapter and reflect upon their own responses to the questions provided prior to each meeting. Each session can then be organized around questions such as:

1. How did the stories within this chapter resonate with or contrast to your own mid-life experience?

2. What did you learn about your own spiritual crisis and joy as you answered the questions?

3. What scriptures or other resources do you find particularly meaningful as you contemplate this aspect of your mid-life spiritual development?

4. How can we as a group support one another in our next steps in our mid-life spiritual journeys?

When I thanked people at the conclusion of the interviews, they would insist on thanking *me* for the chance to think through and talk about the questions. They would say things like "It's just so good to talk with someone else about all of this." This reinforces my feeling that there are too few places where we feel invited to enter into meaningful dialogue about the things that matter most in life—and it is a relief when we get the chance. My hope is that this book will provide a catalyst and resource for such dialogue.

# 1
# Net Worth

> **"The day will arrive in his life when work—devotion to work, work's steady pressure and application—will be all that stands between himself and the bankruptcy of his soul."**
>
> *Carol Shields*, Larry's Party

*I* was excited about showing our new home to my mother and aunt. We had taken possession of a lovely flower garden and a few mature trees. It was July and, with great pride, I presented our prolific mountain ash. The tree was lush and loaded with clusters of bright orange berries. I waited to hear their expressions of admiration and instead heard gasps of shock and concern. As experienced gardeners they saw a tree in trouble. Its productivity was not a sign of health or well-being but an indication that the tree was in distress.

I had assumed that the tree's blatant excess was a good thing—a sure sign that all was good. I realize now that I was looking at the tree with the typical values of a late–twentieth-century North American. After months of reflecting upon the nature of mid-life, I have come to see this tree as a teacher about the relationship between productivity and the mid-life experience.

The three of us began cutting off and discarding branches with great urgency in that otherwise calm summer moment. Even with radical surgery, my aunt cautioned me, it was not at all clear that the tree would survive the winter that was to follow. In the early spring I anxiously watched and waited. There were no visible signs of life but eventually, as late spring unfolded, blossoms and then berries began to appear again. The tree has survived, though it is not the same. It is healthy but with a new look, and there were not quite as many berries the following summer. It would not likely have survived without being pruned on that day in July.

Productivity is how most of us in North American culture have measured our worth and our well-being. Well-being has meant well-doing. What do you do? What have you accomplished? How much do you make? What outward signs are there of your accomplishments and productivity? These are the questions that lie under much of what we say about anyone's identity and value.

In the film, *A Civil Action,* a personal injury lawyer takes a case on behalf of parents who are worried that children in their town have fallen sick as a result of contaminated water in local wells. The lawyer, played by John Travolta, pays a high price for his growing obsession to find the root of the problem. At the end he finds himself in court, filing for bankruptcy, and the judge (played by Kathy Bates) says to him: "After seventeen years practising law, all you have to show for it is $14.00 in a chequing account and a portable radio? Where did it all go—the property, the bank accounts—the things by which one measures one's life?"

The things by which one measures one's life are redefined numerous times during any lifetime. But measuring one's life is an inevitable task of mid-life. After years of investing in the judge's kind of measurements and in its accompanying myth of meaning, many mid-lifers feel empty, whether or not our bank accounts are full. Whatever myths we've embraced about who we are during the first part of our lives do not seem to satisfy anymore.

*How have you measured your life up to this point? How might you want to measure your life from here to the end?*

We are also starting from the other end of the measuring tape. A mid-life friend recently said to me, "I no longer want to base my work and meaning on my life up to this point; instead, I want to live and work with the end of life as my guide." This is the stage at which we realize that our lives are limited and we think about our legacy.

Making our way in the external world is an important focus for us in the first journey of our life. Dr. Al Evans is an ordained minister of The United Church of Canada, a psychologist and professor who has worked a great deal in the areas of family therapy and suicide studies. He told me,

From infancy to the mid-thirties a person is involved in the first journey of life. Mainly it is a journey in which the individual lives outside of him- or herself: getting an education; learning to relate and communicate with those outside of the family; developing independence; fitting into the adult world; finding a job, a place of his or her own, a mentor; and establishing a home and family.

As I look back, I see a continuous and connected unfolding of my work and sense of meaning in my twenties and thirties. Hard work produced experience and results. It seemed that anything was possible. I was somehow driven to do well and to prove myself in a succession of jobs and challenges. Coming from an activist Protestant tradition ensured that "changing the world" was forever front and centre on my personal "to do" list. I was certain that I was chipping away at it. Opportunities followed one another like connected rose petals, opening and unfolding. There seemed to be an inherent order to it all, and others my age also seemed to focus on their blooming. Not that it was all easy. It involved a lot of struggle, but we seemed somehow to thrive on the difficulties and challenges. We blossomed and made our mark in one way or another.

But in my forties the rose began to fade. I found myself questioning what I had really accomplished after all. The world did not look changed by my efforts. By many external measures I was successful, juggling the demands of work inside and outside of the home and reviewing what I knew others saw as a long list of accomplishments. I had developed a small consulting business around some television work and much of it was based upon values that I hold dear. Doing on-air presentation with three different networks meant that much of my work was visible, so others often buttressed my wavering sense of accomplishment with praise and thanks. But the internal doubts meant that the rose no longer looked as beautiful *to me*. What had I really accomplished after all? What did any of it amount to? For the first time in my life I did not have a clue of what might naturally come next. I was in mid-life.

All the petals were fully open and there was no sign of more to come. The pattern of growth had to change dramatically and petals were due to fall.

In a total shock to the system, like the pruning of a rose bush, I was suddenly cut off from the work I thought I loved the most. The organization for which I had worked for twenty-one years no longer needed me for a regular piece of work I'd been doing at that time. I was forty-four years old and I had no option but to discover a new sense of meaning and of work. It was a crisis and a blessing. And, as I look back now, I know that there would have been no new blossoms unless the bush had been pruned, one way or another.

I have learned that this is a common mid-life experience. Any number of things ignite fires of self-examination at this stage, but we are engulfed in their heat and smoke most often in relation to our work—in relation to the things we do that have given meaning to our lives.

In research for this book, my own experience led me to ask questions such as:

- What identity questions are raised for the first time in mid-life?
- What answers are no longer sufficient and where are satisfying answers to be found?

I took these and many other questions into my interviews with a variety of mid-lifers. Some who spoke with me said it was a promotion that caused them mid-life angst; for others it was losing their jobs. The kids leaving home, failing health, the death of a parent, and crises in close relationships are other triggers that are the focus of later chapters. One way or another, it became clear from all of the people I spoke with that no one can expect a smooth, continuous transition from the work of early adulthood into work, worth, and meaning as a mid-lifer.

My conversations with others in mid-life, and with teachers and counsellors gave me some helpful perspectives on what is happening here, as well as more questions and where some good answers are to be found.

Professor Al Evans explains that it was a researcher by the name of Elliot Jaques who first coined the phrase "mid-life crisis" from his observations of artists and composers. Jaques watched creative geniuses go through critical transitions beginning in their mid-thirties. Some made dramatic changes and, as a result, saw their true creative capacity emerge for the first time; some burned out creatively or died; some made a smoother transition to a very different style from that which they had practised before their mid-thirties.

The greatest challenge seemed to be to face the pruning shears in order to ensure that new life—rather than stagnation or death—resulted from their cut. Mid-life offers the promise of a very creative time, of making way for even lovelier blossoms than before, but if we try to escape the pain of growth, then withering and decline, even the death of creativity and spirit are definite possibilities.

*What threats to your spiritual life do you have to deal with? Where can you see new life?*

Mid-lifers described to me at least two kinds of crisis shaped by our culture's high value on incessant productivity. First, there are those who are running so hard to continue being productive—despite their age and some increasing physical limitations—that they live under a relentless burden of stress. They no longer want to run so hard. They know their spiritual lives are in trouble but feel trapped by so many obligations and can see no other way. They feel buried and lost.

There are also those who are no longer productive in the ways they were in their earlier years. Parents who provided meals, cleaned laundry, and cared for young children are no longer needed to provide this care. Workers have found that their work has disappeared due to changes in the workplace, including layoffs. Employees who no longer see the value in what they produce are not putting their hearts into it or getting the results they did previously.

In some ways, life's first journey presents us with relatively straightforward definitions of work. Parenting is one illustration. When my boys were babies, my job description and related worth as a parent were clear: feed them, clean them, cuddle them, and such. But as they grew, my parenting work became increasingly more subtle and complex. The rhythm of holding just enough and letting go just enough has been constant but the physical, visible work I do in my role as parent has consistently diminished. Even though my work as a parent is not finished, I have to adjust to a radically reduced role and deal with the resulting questions of value and worth. The fruits of my labour are young men who are able to step out and make their own way in the world. Like so many other kinds of mid-life work, parental worth is now more rooted in subtleties than in visible gestures. It is not an easy transition.

My conversation with Al Evans set the stage for understanding what our questions about identity, worth, and meaning are all about at mid-life. At seventy-eight, he thinks of himself as being in the late stages of mid-life.

I've just finished writing a book, I'm starting to write another one and I expect I'll be writing in my eighties. I swim every morning and feel very well. But when I turned forty I found that a disturbing time. My really creative years started when I was in my early fifties. I really started to put everything together in my fifties and that has continued— creating courses, writing books, doing research, and becoming a grandfather.

As far as one's spiritual life goes, mid-life is probably the richest time. We have thought about death earlier in our lives but as Daniel Levinson says, there's a significant change here, when we ask "Now that I'm doing what I *should* be doing, what do I *want* to do with my life?"

(This wasn't the first I'd heard of mid-life fatigue as being a "should." Maturity brings with it a courage to question others' expectations.)

Levinson suggests that the reason a person shifts from outer productivity to inner meaning lies in the simple realization that life doesn't go on forever.

Evans says that the rate of suicide triples at mid-life and starts to increase from there. Depression and narcissism are problems. People start to feel guilty, angry, exasperated, and trapped. As a person deals with these issues, he or she starts to deal with soul issues. There is great potential for a conversion experience that comes of this. When a person faces issues, conversion to new life is possible. But opting for denial or getting drunk, sick, or killing oneself are sometimes chosen instead.

You can't just say "I want to have a spiritual experience," but you can open yourself up. Spirituality is an energy found in all humans which drives and enables them to respond creatively to the meta-needs of the individual in order to become fully human.

I like Evans' definition of spirituality and believe that when he talks about meta-needs he is talking about meeting transcendent needs such as finding joy and peace and awareness of the wonders beyond what we can see and touch. In every conversation with mid-lifers I was very aware that I was speaking with a spiritual person. These folks knew from experience that there was a lot more to life than shopping. They certainly knew that what they were looking for could not be bought. In earlier years they had come to know and play by the rules of the outside world; now was the time to begin journeying towards a less visible form of security and peace.

And yet Evans' spirituality still cares for the world and other beings. He suggests that if the central question of mid-life is about meaning, then at the end of each day, it is helpful to ask oneself "What have I done today that is meaningful?" And if you get to the point in your life where you say "I haven't done anything of meaning for anyone and it's too late and I can't change," this is the core of a mid-life crisis.

We are our own harshest critics and given that mid-life is a self-reflective time, thoughts often seem to turn to self-criticism. While this may hold the promise of good change, it can also produce self-loathing, destructiveness, and stagnation. If I can only see what is wrong with me, I may lose hope for any new possibilities.

Evans describes four steps to growth and change in contrast to stagnation:

1. Be aware of yourself.

2. Understand why you are there and what has taken you to that place.

3. Forgive—ask for and give forgiveness.

4. Pursue intimacy with others and with God that will lead to redemption and becoming the person you want to be.

> I remember working with a man who was the president of a multinational company. He was a very powerful man and he had been referred to me by a psychiatrist who couldn't help him. He was suicidal and depressed and *I* couldn't help him. I went to England for a time and didn't see him until eight to ten years later. I was surprised when I did see him. He looked vibrant. He had changed dramatically. I grabbed hold of him, we sat down and I asked him what had happened to him. He listed four things:
> First, he had quit his job—that wonderful job with a lot

of money, power and status—and had opened his own little store.

Second, he had made a friend—he had always been closed and arrogant.

Third, he felt that things were going well for him and that he needed to give something back so he decided to volunteer at the hospital.

Fourth, when his life had opened up with his work, his intimate relationship, and the way he was connecting with society, he suddenly had a feeling that somebody else had visited him. It was like a spiritual experience so he went to a priest and asked the priest what was happening to him. This was the fourth important thing he did and by this time he was about sixty. He joined the church and nurtured this experience there.

He used his mid-life crisis to grow. If he hadn't done that, he would have been dead because neither the psychiatrist nor I could help him.

From Professor Evans (and others) I have learned that unprecedented questions about meaning are at the heart of mid-life work on identity. I have also learned that the ways a mid-life person responds to these questions can result either in new life and creativity or in physical or psychological death.

From my own guided spiritual explorations and conversations I have come to the conclusion that we all enter this world to do important work but that work may not be what our society has told us it is. During the first half of our lives we tend to accept socially defined images of ourselves and throw ourselves into fulfilling them. But when we begin to question our work as defined by others and begin to take spiritual reference points seriously, joyful possibilities unfold.

*At the end of today, ask yourself "What have I done today that is meaningful?"*

Scholar and teacher Joseph Campbell spoke about how sad it is when someone climbs to the top of the ladder only to discover that it was leaning against the wrong wall. Feeling that we have had the ladder against the wrong wall appears to be a common mid-life experience. And other walls of the world do not look immediately appealing. There seems to be a universal sense of need to look beyond the walls to a larger calling.

The thirtieth chapter of the book of Deuteronomy describes God setting before us life or death and telling us to choose life in order to live in the love of God. Mid-life seems to be when the call finally gets through: let go of ladders to success that have not led to fulfillment and choose instead that which is life-giving work for you.

Being at the top of the ladder is a lot like being fully in bloom. There are no more upward steps and no more petals to unfold. When I was there at forty-four, the only source of help and perspective was spiritual. It is not that God's spirit had been absent from earlier calls to vocational choices but now listening to God was my *only* option. I no longer trusted any other authorities when it came to determining my life's work from here.

Listening to God and choosing life has a good deal to do with what developmental theorist Erik Erikson called generativity—evaluating how our behaviour has contributed to community, society, and the earth itself. While we may have been passionate about righting society's wrongs in our early adulthood, caring for others' health and even for the health of the earth itself seems now to be essential to the health of our own souls. We are now caring because we have been told that it is the right thing to do. We now care about what we are contributing because we're listening to a more ultimate, deeper authority that is gently teaching us that our life depends on it.

This theme of generativity is playfully developed in a number of stories within Allan Chinen's book of classic stories and mythic tales, *Once upon a Midlife*. I particularly like his stories of characters who do not want to die—then they are confronted with what life without death would be like. In one story, a millionaire who is mysteriously given the gift of immortality eventually grows to hate it. When given another chance at a normal life—including death—he takes it and follows the advice given with it: "Work hard, raise your children well, provide for their future, and help your neighbors. Then you will fear death no more."

John is one of the mid-lifers who agreed to talk with me about his sense of work and worth. He is now a fifty-two-year-old financial planner. He was laid off as an institutional money broker in the first wave of North American corporate layoffs that eventually crashed to shore in the early 1990s. He was thirty-nine when the ladder was pulled out from under him. He described his experience to me:

> In corporate life, forty is pretty much a cutting point. If you're not moving up, you're moved aside. It's often difficult to see a silver lining on the cloud when you lose your job. We think, "Oh, this is terrible," and it *is* terrible. I was the single supporter of the family and we'd just had a third child. My job was highly specialized, there were no other jobs around, and I had untransferable skills. That twelve to fifteen months out of a job was a walk in the wilderness which I now reflect on as very beneficial. I talked to a whole range of people through networking and a universal theme was how sadly unhappy most people are in corporate life. It was drudgery—a means to an end—and this came as a real eye-opener for me. It enabled me to think more about myself, and I realized that I hadn't been happy either. Here was an opportunity to change that even though it wasn't an easy transition.
>
> That's how I became self-employed and now I wish I'd done it sooner. It was also a great test of character because you've got to start again. It's not humiliating but it's humbling to go back and knock on doors—in whatever sense you're doing it in life. You're starting over in proving your worth to people. Above all I think I learned how to cope with adversity and I think that was a blessing.

John spoke at length about how this time of relative isolation was a great opportunity to take stock and to look at the truth about himself and at what gifts he had that he was called to use in some new way. He chose life over death: accepting what he learned about his weaknesses as well as his strengths; accepting the risks of self-employment when returning to a corporate job would have been easier; opening himself to spiritual guidance.

> At the end of the day God as spirit is there. There is a power that will see you through but it's not chicken soup or

"happy ever after" in any way. You see it incrementally, with slow progress. I remember talking with a psychologist years later, after my wife died of cancer, and he said that in such difficult times, you have to find one little thing to cling onto like a little nail-hold on a cliff face. You just need something that you can dig into and leverage from. It might be as simple as doing some business you weren't expecting to do. And you will never grow unless you make mistakes— probably a lot of them. In corporate life you're damned if you make mistakes. In fact, you're being paid not to make mistakes. I can grow more quickly in my self-employment than I ever could in a corporate environment.

Similarly, in my own case, it was in self-employment when I truly heard Jesus' words for me about God's care for the lilies of the field and the birds of the air. I was loved and, one way or another—in the midst of not knowing what I would be doing tomorrow—God would care for me. Earlier I had placed my security in my job and now it was more properly placed.

Once centred in God's love, God's guidance seems clearer. If we are no longer automatically accepting others' definition of work and meaning, we get to figure it out according to our own values and a sense of deeper direction. The courage comes. Here is how it works for John.

I have to feel that what I'm doing matters—that when people leave a meeting or a gathering I've been involved in, they're better for it. They may not be happier but they're better for it because I've told them the truth. In my work as a financial planner, especially, I think it's very important to give people the truth and I don't think that's what con- temporary society wants to deliver. So, for example, one walks this awkward path of telling people they have to modify their material expectations. This troubles them because they're perpetually nurtured with this idea of an onward and upward rise in material acquisitiveness.

When people are younger they have two major pre- occupations: wealth and health. When they get older, it's the

same two things but inverted: health and wealth, and health
is defined in all kinds of ways: spiritual, mental, or physical.
The idea that material wealth will contribute to one's well-
being becomes minimal. The total absence of it is painful so
I'm not advocating poverty, but people with money
probably become more neurotic about it. People come to
me and say "I want you to do these things with my money"
and I say to them "What do you want to do with your life?
Then we can talk about your money." It's a challenging
question but I think it matters and it's about stewardship.

A quest for integrity is a strong mid-life theme, evident in John's story.
Integrity developed as he travelled through his wilderness, took stock
of his strengths and weaknesses, and found a way of working that is
consistent with his values and beliefs. John grew up in a strong British
Methodist tradition that has influenced him profoundly. He reads his
Bible every day but no longer has a regular church involvement. He
reflects upon how Jesus himself spent a lot of time outside his organized
religion yet was also intimately connected to the synagogue. Sorting out
his relationship with a community of faith is a lively question for John.
He finds that church services do not offer him enough emphasis on
prayer.

A new or renewed emphasis on meditation and prayer was frequently
raised in conversation with mid-lifers. Those who found earlier meaning
in the more active, external dimensions of religious life and work said
they no longer found this satisfying without an accompanying intimacy
with the source of all that activity. And those who had valued contemplative thought during the first part of their journey, now sought greater
focus and accompanying consistency in action.

A woman who had a rich internal life as an early mid-lifer told me
that she became impatient with her circles of thought that were out-
wardly unproductive. While prayer continues to be important to her,
she has made a shift in emphasis from inner work to outer prayer work,
towards greater consistency and balance. Accompanying her daughter to
a gay pride parade is, for example, a new and productive form of prayer
for her. She still needs to find quiet before and after these great events but
loves the strong sense of people in the crowd being her brothers, sisters,

sons, and daughters. For her, mid-life prayer needed to become active and involved in the world she can see and touch, as well as in her inner world.

Coming to terms with one's own religious roots emerged as another frequent theme. Many had left their traditional practices but felt incomplete without something to replace them. Some found new religious community and practice in mid-life. Others returned to their religious homes with a new heart. Sherry is one of those who felt she had to leave and then, much later, felt she had to return. Once again, this decision took place in the midst of tumultuous vocational discernment.

Sherry pays close attention to what she describes as signs. Her most recent job was as a senior manager with a major bank. Before that she worked for a half-dozen corporations. Sherry is fifty-one and has been laid off twice. By paying attention to a number of divine nudgings, she has found an exciting way through it all. Just over nine years ago Sherry had stopped going to church because she felt that it was unhealthy to be in church while hating the experience of Sunday worship. Then one weekend she attended an event sponsored by a downtown workplace ministry and it became the weekend of what she now calls her spiritual awakening: "I just knew I had to be there. I had a spiritual void, except that I didn't know what a spiritual void was."

Sherry has travelled a long way since that weekend. She has formed an organization called Centre for Spirituality at Work and plans a return to corporate life with a new set of skills and insights. She is studying at a Jesuit college even though she knew nothing about the Jesuits until she saw a whole set of signs directing her to consider this particular college. She reports that finally, after being interviewed to be a student there, "All of a sudden there was such an overpowering sense of the presence of God that it was several minutes before I could move or speak. I knew that this is what I needed to do." Her employer had given her the option of either outplacement counselling or financial support for re-training and when she asked about the money available for training, it was exactly what she needed for her two years' tuition. She saw another sign.

Sherry has an MBA in marketing and this course will give her an MA in ministry and spirituality. She plans to integrate what she has learned in obtaining these two degrees to consult with individuals wanting to connect spirit with work individually and with executives who want to do things in their workplace to address vocational discernment; issues of values and ethics, of teamwork, of climate and workplace environment, of work/life balance, and of decision-making. She echoes mid-life themes of risking to do work that has integrity and of having the sense of being held and cared for as she risks. She is sure to have a lot of mid-life clients!

> I've let go of attachments in the sense that I now recognize that the significant things in life are very much part of a divine purpose that is not for me to control but for me to be open to. It's all about openness, alertness, discernment, and being ready to take action, but recognizing that the purpose is beyond myself so, when it comes to relationships with significant others and with work, there's a feeling of freedom because it's not all on me.

Sherry's words closely parallel what Al Evans described as a mid-life spiritual openness.

> It's also a release from everything having to be rational. We are each an integration of body and spirit. I come from a very rational place. I'm a strong thinker and that is my nature. This is probably a mid-life issue for me but it takes time to learn the other side of thinking and to integrate that because that only comes through experience. I'm aware in corporate workplaces of the dominance and the limitations of rationality. When you start becoming more fully who you are there's a release and joy in that. The greatest abandonment is to let things happen and to accept co-creation.

Sherry's point, that mid-life is a time for achieving greater balance and integration, is a significant one. In mid-life we seem drawn towards exploring ways of being that present a contrasting counterbalance to how we have lived out the first part of our journey. The drive towards integrating opposing poles such as reliance on the head and reliance on the heart is something we will explore more closely in the chapter called The Personals.

Sherry's experience also reinforces the mid-life sense of importance in paying attention to signs and opportunities that come from beyond our control and of being open to co-creation with something greater than ourselves. She described her spirituality as two-fold, based in her connection with God and in the tangible fruits that result from that connection. She has let go of an earlier need to control her life and now focuses upon staying open to what will come and being ready to act upon whatever opportunities God gives.

*What attachments may be getting in the way of you being open, alert, and discerning of signs pointing to your future? How can you put them in their proper place in order to remain open?*

Even before the loss of employment shocked her into a new path, Sherry learned a valuable lesson from what began as a traumatic event.

Late one night while I was still employed, I was mugged on my way home. By the time I stopped chasing the thieves—who got away easily on bikes—I realized I was in a rough neighbourhood. A First Nations man saw me and offered me all of the money in his pocket. He said he was a street person so he'd be all right, but I'd need the money to get home. The next morning when I arrived at my office the receptionist told me that a man had brought in my purse which had been found in a schoolyard. My business card was inside so he brought it to my office. When I got home that night there was a message from a woman who's the cook at a nearby drop-in centre and women's hostel. I went to see her and learned that she and the people who prepare a breakfast program for kids there were the ones who had found my purse and gathered up all of my stuff. I went home, bundled up sheets and towels and got a pot of flowers to take back to them to thank them. The man who had first helped me when I was mugged had told me which hostel he lived in so I also took a thank-you card and some money to him. Then on Sunday morning I woke up with the most overpowering feeling. I had to go to church but I didn't know where to go because I hadn't attended anywhere for quite sometime. I remembered someone telling me

about a church they liked and so I went there and the
sermon spoke to me so much that I stayed for the second
service which spoke to me even more deeply. I've been there
ever since.

Sherry's attentiveness to signs led her to find spiritual nourishment in
the church again, but this time with a more intimate relationship with
God, which she had craved.

On one of my darkest days of wondering about the meaning of my
own life, two things happened. I visited a mid-life friend who was living
with advanced cancer and I bumped into another long-distant friend
who had just had a book published. My first friend gave me perspective
on what's really important in life (not "high grades" as she put it) and
how precious every day is. Being with her took me out of myself to being
more open to the kind of connection with God that Sherry described.
On my way home from the hospital I met up with my other friend in a
surprise encounter. She pulled a copy of her book out of her bag and
autographed it for me with the comment "To Mardi, who has left her
mark." God got my attention. Like Sherry, I opened my eyes to a sign. I
could let go of my obsession about figuring out how to leave my mark
because apparently I already had. With every new step along the mid-life
journey, I'm becoming more attentive to and trusting of such signs of
love, guidance, and grace.

Ralph has found life-giving answers to questions of meaning as a
result of becoming a Sikh, with the help of Babaji, an Indian guru. Ralph
grew up in a Jewish family in New York City. He loves Judaism and as a
child could frequently be found looking for God behind the curtains—
behind the ark—in the synagogue. "There is nothing wrong with
Judaism and I don't think any less of it now. I found my way to God
[through becoming a Sikh] and began practising within a tradition that
affirmed everything I learned as a child.

At fifty years of age—at mid-life—I see that learning
how to live never ends. God is the ultimate teacher and you
sit in class every day, trying to learn from mistakes, begging
for forgiveness, and trying not to make them again. I have a
wife and two beautiful boys, a job, a house, a mortgage, cars

and payments and the same things everybody else does. Since my days as a graduate student, I've now had twenty-two years of a good dose of western materialism. But still, there is much more peace now than when I was a young adult. I describe peace in relation to video games: you clear the first level, breathe a sigh of relief, and then they come at you again, fast and furious at the next level. You get about two seconds to breathe in between each level.

By mid-life we have been blessed with experience and perspective as Ralph demonstrates. Put simply, we have lots of stuff to look back on. I do not remember ever before being so intently aware of my own life's stages as I am in mid-life. Stage theory has interested me since my twenties but it was only theory before. I smile at Ralph's image of life as a video game but it is apt. When one set of threats is put to rest and when one set of lessons has been learned we have enough historical perspective to know that we will be presented with new ones. We count on spiritual strength gained from what has gone before because we will indeed need it in each new level, even within mid-life itself. There is a peace that comes from knowing that we have been accompanied through what has gone before and will not be abandoned now. Ralph had more to say about that peace.

We make a huge mistake if we think that spiritual peace is synonymous with material success—that if we have glitches in our business relationships, for example, that we're not blessed. If we simply look at all kinds of religious leaders who we see as reflections of God's power, they demonstrate that worldly suffering is nothing and that we rise above it. Very often worldly crises lead us back to our spiritual roots. They provide us with the opportunity to be shaken back to seeing what it's all about. There's then more peace because we're learning to let it flow through us, letting the ego get out of the way. It's how you perceive and react to problems that defines your spiritual growth. By mid-life you're at a harder level but hopefully your faith is stronger—not to tempt God as the devil tried to tempt Jesus—but to feel God's hand holding you. This hand has carried you so far

and guided you through untold difficulties. You have
become stronger in God.

Ralph echoes the importance of meditation to the mid-life soul.

> When we clean our house in the darkness, we don't see
> the cobwebs. Meditation turns on the light so that we can
> see what we need to do. But if it only affects us individually,
> it has no value. God's not giving us a light to keep under a
> bushel. God is reaching out to us. It is part of God's plan to
> reach out and raise people to see the light. Without people
> like Babaji, the prophet Mohammed, Jesus, and other
> teachers, you can't imagine that light in the world. As more
> people share the light, you become more conscious of it.

I began daily meditation almost a year ago and it has enabled me to
bring greater energy and focus to everything I do. I have a deeper sense of
not being alone and of being connected and guided. My spiritual director
started me off with a simple Christian mantra that helps to quiet my
mind and imagine myself absorbing God's love. By taking time for this in
the morning, I increase the chances of reflecting that love during the day.

Tony practises meditation within a different set of circumstances than
anyone I have yet described. Tony believes that the function of mid-life is
to take personal responsibility. But he is not talking about a job or work
in the way most people talk about responsibility. At fifty-two he has been
through many difficult times and is now on a disability pension. In fact,
he does not expect ever to work in a job again. He has taught high
school, had an electronics business that failed, and returned to agri-
culture, which he knew best from his family roots. But eventually the
physical toll from diabetes and heart attacks led to another business
failure and inability to work. As a result of a kidney transplant he is no
longer on dialysis, but insulin has caused him eye problems. He has dealt
with numerous surgeries and has been intimately acquainted with the
prospect of death.

> I lost most of my money and had to go on disability
> pension. I tried to get back to work several times but with

dialysis I was told to forget it. There was a lot of time for introspection and asking "Why me?" I came to the conclusion that financial and material success wasn't for me. I'd been in and out of it several times and it wasn't necessary for me to have that kind of success. Despite our best efforts we're not always in control of our lives. But you don't see your whole world collapse and not get depressed.

From within his depression, Tony returned to his religious roots. He had grown up in a Hindu home in Trinidad and knows now that it's one of the few countries in the world where it is commonplace to enter a home to see pictures of Jesus Christ, Krishna, and Hindu divinities all together on the wall. Everyone celebrated every religious festival during his boyhood. Even as a Hindu he attended Sunday school in a Presbyterian church and attended services with friends in Catholic and Anglican churches and at the Mosque. His father supported the Presbyterian church with donations at harvest time. Tony still finds it strange to live in a country [Canada] where religious identities are mutually exclusive. He says, "God didn't sign up on any religion. He doesn't belong to them—they belong to him."

I turned myself around and went back to Hinduism and also studied Buddhism, Zen, and things like that. I decided that I needed to do my own research and in my case that meant meditation. Meditation gave me a whole new perspective. I understand that despite all of our best efforts, we are not the ones who determine what will happen. Everyone should try to be the best they can be but I don't believe in original sin. I believe in karma and reincarnation and that the universe is so situated that nothing goes unpunished or unrewarded. Everything comes back to personal responsibility.

Tony presents an intriguing mixture. On the one hand he demonstrates a mid-life acceptance that he cannot control the circumstances of his life; on the other hand, he believes that this is the time for accepting personal responsibility. He feels mid-life is not a time for throwing up one's hands and giving up, even when things are hard. It is a time for understanding the difference thoughts and attitudes—and even the smallest acts—can make to the world. Even though he is limited by severe physical problems and few material resources, Tony has done a lot of volunteer work in adult literacy and provides peer support to other kidney transplant recipients.

This reinforces another characteristic of how mid-life is different from the earlier part of our journey. We have accumulated experience and wisdom built on that experience, which we did not have at a younger age. As Tony demonstrates, we have knowledge and pragmatism, refined by adversity. The more years of difficulty one has had, the greater one's potential for bringing gifts of understanding.

> If I were given the chance to go back and trade my experiences I wouldn't because I am now closer to God than I would ever have been able to be if I hadn't gone through these things. Steel is made from iron ore and it has to go through fire before it becomes steel.
>
> When I was younger I didn't even think about these things. I tended to look more at material gains and immediate satisfaction. I guess people who haven't gone through difficult times are often still like that. I see people who have to occupy themselves 100 percent of the time with busy hands and busy brains. Some of these people are brilliant in that they're filled with facts but they don't have knowledge. The one person they don't know is themself. They avoid getting to know themselves. The most significant line to me in the Bible is "Be still and know that I am God."
>
> God is everywhere and everywhere is God. In meditation you raise your own mental vibration to distract and direct the mind to receive more divine thoughts. And one of the most powerful forces in the world is thought. Thoughts are like radio waves and since nothing in the universe is wasted, my goal is to broadcast good thoughts. The first way to change the world is to think the way you'd like the world to think.

Tony is no longer physically capable of being productive in the ways most people see productivity. He has, however, taken responsibility for his life and found deep meaning as a result of choosing and nurturing life out of the ashes of failure, physical limitation, and depression. Choosing cynicism would have been understandable but it would have been a choice for death. Tony chose life. In Evans' terms, he paid attention to an energy that has driven and enabled him to respond creatively to the greater needs of himself and others, to become fully human.

*How are you faced with a choice of life or death?*

His sense of responsibility even extends to *how* he thinks. I imagine that when he was younger he may have been more agitated about dealing with daily racism. His conviction remains strong and yet gentle, mellowed by mid-life.

> I've been struck by seeing people make judgments of others on the basis of religion and colour. When scientists are studying the properties of something, they apply as many instruments as possible before coming to conclusions. But somebody who is racist makes a judgment based only on appearance. It's as if I gave you a video camera to tape your vacation in Hawaii with all of its beauty and colour and you came back and insisted on watching it in black and white.

In all these stories—John's discernment of a new vocation, Sherry's openness to signs of spiritual direction, Ralph's commitment to daily spiritual learning, Tony's learning to rise above crippling physical limitations—we see people discovering a net worth they had not previously known or imagined.

The first part of our lives has pushed us out into the world as a rose bush is pushed out from the ground. We build on inherited growth, but it is only after a beautiful crop of buds bloom into full-grown blossoms that we experience the pain of having it all cut away to make way for what is new and often better. The process may be either dramatic or gradual but to deal well with its questions of meaning and worth, the mid-life soul must be open to conversion to new life. Old growth will need to be cut away and die.

Such transitions are never easy and indeed they are most often traumatic. Surviving them—and going on to thrive in new life—requires that we have the strength to let go. In our next chapter we will hear more about letting go.

2

# *Letting Go*

**"Getting older was to witness the steady decline of limitless possibility. That's all it was."**

*Carol Shields,* Larry's Party

*I*t was amazing how often the theme of "letting go" came up in my conversations with other mid-lifers—letting go of burdensome possessions, ambitions, expectations; of the exuberance of youth; of the presence of loved ones. Whether we are forced or inspired to let go of things that have seemed fundamental to our lives so far, they are now cast in a new light—and often cast overboard.

Letting go of the ability to work from dawn to midnight with the capacity to simultaneously manage so many more ideas and projects than I now can, has been difficult. I have always liked variety but I can no longer do well in as many areas of endeavour as I believe I once did. I have had to slow down and choose my priorities while letting go of things I would also like to do.

I have had to let go of some dreams and ambitions too. I notice that I have not changed the world as much as my twenty-year-old self thought that I would have by now. But there are compensations. I am content with smaller assignments and satisfied with more modest results. I know the significance of delivering a casserole, providing a word of encouragement to someone in need of it, presenting a well-prepared eulogy, or taking time to pray. These did not seem so significant to me when I was a younger adult, always in motion!

In many cases people have spoken to me of letting go of burdensome "shoulds" whether they've come from others or from within themselves: shoulds associated with being a perfect parent or a perfect child, with trying to make our parents or children perfect, or with trying to be at the top of our field of work.

And being forced to let go of the physical presence of parents, partners, and friends is an increasingly frequent experience in the mid-life journey. It has not been easy to let go of my father's gregarious earthly presence or of the dream of one more good conversation with a friend who has fallen to cancer. I have not had a choice about letting go of what might have been in these precious relationships.

Margaret Fisher Brillinger is a therapist and adult educator who has worked with individuals and families in all stages of life. She reflects upon how her thinking shifted with her own experience of mid-life:

> I remember leading a workshop in my thirties and saying "You can do it all—you just have to figure out when and how to manage it all." But I know now that it doesn't work that way because the forks in the road come and we have to make choices. We cannot go back and take the other road later on, because that one is gone and the forks keep coming. Mid-life is a time when we realize that life is subtractive rather than additive and that life is short. We've got to make choices, so it's a time of reassessing and soul-searching. For me that's what the Spirit is all about. This is my one shot at it and I need to make as much meaning of what I'm called to do as possible, to make sure I'm really doing what I'm called to do and that I'm really on track.

By mid-life we have learned a few things about how to let go because we have already experienced death in some measure. And every death results in grief, whether it is the death of a relationship, a role, a pattern, or a habit. The experience of having survived grief in the past could reassure and guide us through new experiences of grief, but as Margaret suggests, we still often resist what we need to do.

> Throughout our lives we have to learn how to let go because any change, by definition, means that we're saying good-bye to one thing to take on another. Our acquisitive, western approach, however, tends to suggest that life is just

more, more, more. We add on, and a lot of our stress is based on not understanding the side of change that's about letting go. We think we can continue adding on and tend to do what I call "elastic living." We will add on another friend, without stopping to say, "If I take on this new friend, what old friend will I have less time for?" We become like elastic bands to the point where we have no elasticity left to accommodate surprises, so we get stressed out or physically ill. We call this state by different names.

There's emotion involved in any change of roles. When I'm no longer the active, involved parent, for example, I have to stand back and watch my children make their own decisions. I can no longer make decisions for them and protect them. I like Erma Bombeck's description of how children are like kites. We let the string out and they go higher and higher. A part of us is so proud, excited, and delighted and another part of us is so sad because the kite gets further away as it rises.

Letting go of hourly, daily parenting is turning out to be one of my biggest mid-life difficulties. Like most parents, this is the job I have invested in the most. I have protected and coached and organized to the point of exhaustion and fulfillment. And now my kids do not need or want me to do that for them anymore. In fact, I know that the extent to which I try to continue playing the role of a mother to younger children is the extent to which I will inhibit them from fulfilling their life challenges as young adults.

*What roles, patterns or habits do you need to let go?*

Roles may be the hardest things to let go of—roles like parent or spouse or child—when those who have collaborated with us in defining them leave, die, or change in other ways. The parts we play have been developed over many years and with great investment and practice to get them right. No one is standing in the wings with a new script to replace the old. Once we let go, as we must, we have to start from scratch, often feeling empty and disoriented.

Such mid-life moments give us the chance, sometimes for the first time, to think about who decided what role we would take or how we would play it. When I became a mother, my role seemed automatically defined and I did not think much about it. As a parent of young adults, I can no longer do what I did for them when they were young, such as ensure their safety or security in the world. While this leads to deep questioning and frequent uncertainty about how to parent from here, it forces me to look beyond whatever activities and advice I have invested in so far.

I am given the opportunity, in letting go of the past, to think more deeply about the ultimate quality of the parent-child relationship and the values I want it to embody, free of earlier behaviours that no longer fit.

We have already seen that work roles often change at mid-life too— sometimes we are forced from the outside to let go of a kind of work and sometimes the need to let go bubbles up from inside us.

I talked with Susan in her warm living room on a cold winter day, surrounded by old furniture and contemporary art. The room breathed with connections to the past and to something new and emerging. We talked about what she has let go of in relation to work, and in relation to her roles as parent and child.

Susan was a university instructor who let go of teaching to take on writing. She told me about letting go of her love for being active in the world, to make room for a different voice at mid-life—a voice that told her to be more meditative and contemplative and to listen to a call to do more writing. She has let go of grander schemes and come to enjoy what she calls the insignificant and inconsequential nature of her acts.

> For all the grand thoughts I can think of or all the good things I could do—in the long run, what is it really? It is one small breath or one small impulse, but ten years ago I felt it was very significant and very important.

Susan is not saying that her mid-life actions are insignificant compared to those of her youth. On the contrary, she presents one of mid-life's many paradoxes, suggesting that this is the time for having the strength to bear the burden of insight, to see the breakdown in what no longer works and the complexities that must be considered. If we allow enlightenment to accompany the chaos of seeing what is not working, we are enabled to let go and step out of familiar, stagnant ways to take more responsible action.

> I am a conduit, a vessel with things moving through me and if I can let go of enough stuff and baggage, I can be free to remember that I am not the beginning and the end and not responsible for everything. In fact, I can take responsibility because I don't have to be in control.

If we can risk letting go of trying to hold together all of the elements of our lives as we've lived them to date, we can risk embracing chaos and mystery, opening the way for mid-life to be a time of fresh, creative response. Spirit and flesh can come together in a new way, born again.

Susan speculates that depression itself may be a blessing in that it is a call to let go of what is no longer working within us spiritually.

> When I think about our addiction to anti-depressants I wonder about the call of depression itself. Is it the system's own resistance to all of the top-side kind of activity? I think illness, depression, interpersonal breakdown, and vocational crises provide times for breakthrough—as when there's that thin sheaf or line between darkness and daylight when things begin shifting and one becomes aware that there's something else out there.

Night holds the promise of day. But if we are pretending that the night is day, and not acknowledging how tired and bleak we feel, crises will have to pile on top of one another before eventually getting our attention. In order to move on we have to figure out what is holding us back.

In order to let go and become open to a new way, Susan had to reconcile herself with expectations planted firmly inside of her—family expectations that run sturdy and deep.

> I come from a long line of strong, hard-working, rural, faithful Mormons who would say, "But writing doesn't feed a soul, it doesn't clothe a body," and so there's that side of

me that resists it enormously. I've had to develop a strategy for actively forgiving myself when I sit down to write because I feel that I must appease the ancestors—even though there's no one breathing down my neck! I've internalized the mandate to move toward practical, humanitarian activities that bring social benefit in the world but I know that the core of what I can now offer the world grows out of this contemplative side. Allowing this to develop has been important, so I engage in acts of self-forgiveness. When I sit down to write I'm sacrificing some good cause. I'm saying "no" to it for the sake of an essay or a poem that may never see the light of day and that only few people would appreciate.

I've had to let go of ideas of what I should do professionally, moving from the stability of teaching to the anonymity of writing. I've learned that I can let go of what the world says is wise. There are times when I struggle with that but I feel confirmed.

Letting go of what the world says is wise is one of the biggest tasks of mid-life. By now experience has taught us that we can no longer blindly trust the wisdom of others, but the work of uncovering wisdom for ourselves is difficult. Fortunately the years have also provided sufficient strength to face this challenge. We are even finally strong enough to put family directives in their proper perspective.

*What helps you regain balance when old patterns start to break down?*

Still, it is not easy to uncover our own wisdom when submerged in a culture addicted to a narrow set of values that reward constant activity and visible progress. Susan suggests that our whole society desperately needs to examine its preoccupation with busyness, and that mid-lifers are in a position to contribute.

The ability to cultivate a contemplative way in the world is a kind of gift we need at this time as human beings because we have been so used to busyness and production. The ability to cease or resist that and move into a state of

listening and awareness, to dwell with things as opposed to
only exercising stewardship over things, is a very different
sensibility. I think it's a kind of call that exists in all of us to
some degree or another. In exceptional people it may be
there from early in life but for the run-of-the-mill rest of us,
it's something we hear later, when other things start to break
down.

Religion at its best, holds contemplation and action together in
perfect balance. As I reflect upon this now I have more appreciation than
ever for how this can provide people with various stage-appropriate
resources to grow in their faith at different points in their personal life
journeys. The wisdom of the ages can give us sign posts and reference
points beyond ourselves. This is valuable beyond measure when one feels
as if one's life is falling apart.

Although Susan had to let go of some of the prescriptions of her
religious roots in order to develop her contemplative mid-life work, her
spiritual tradition had also, paradoxically, given her a framework in which
to let go of the past.

The beauty of my Mormon tradition is that it's based on
ongoing revelation. I've just taken that and run with it, but
it makes discernment absolutely critical. Otherwise you run
amok. I haven't limited my circle for discernment to the
church but I look for people with a fidelity to truth. And I
go back to the spiritual classics, to Augustine, and to old
masters who spent a long time in those worlds and still have
something to say that's worth listening to. I find a part of
me wakes up when I encounter those voices. For me, there's
still living water there and not enough contemporary voices
like that are being produced.

Susan touches on a resounding mid-life theme. This is a time for
seeking integration and balance. If we have been tipped towards the
expectations and activities of the outside world, we need to let go of that
and attend to what lies inside. And if we have been inwardly focused, it is
time to let go of our private focus to look outward and begin to interact.

In a culture filled with three extroverts (who naturally look outward) for every introvert (who naturally looks inward), it is not surprising that the mid-life desire for balance and integration is more frequently expressed in terms of needing to let go of so much activity to take time for more meditation and reflection.

Susan also describes what "letting go" has meant with reference to her roles in the middle generation, as mother and daughter. A mother of two, she described how having her second child in mid-life was an experience of letting go of perfection.

> My life is chaos now. Whatever aspirations I had of perfection are shot. And there's a mid-life freedom in that. At first it felt like a loss, a letting go of all those things I'd held together that were now starting to crumble. But the further I go into that, the more I feel an enormous freedom to let that chaos be and to not try to hold it all together. I have a terrific desire to keep things humming but I just can't do it anymore and letting go of that feels really good.

Accepting that we cannot actually control our children's world appears to be a mid-life awakening. Susan discovered that by consciously releasing the need to control, she can accept the chaos as a fine place to be.

Her mother, on the other hand, let go of Susan. Long before she died, her emotional illness drove her to push Susan and others from her life. Accepting the chaos that resulted from her mother's letting go of her was more difficult for Susan. She had to let go of being nurtured by the one who was supposed to be the nurturer forever.

> I've had to let go of lots of resentments and of an image of what my relationship with my mother could have been like. I had to let go of the idea that my family would ever be reconciled.
>
> The stuff I went through with my mom was very difficult. She was extremely paranoid and in the last ten years of her life all family members were demonized. The mother-daughter relationship was broken and there was the most protracted period of grief without any way for

reconciliation. When the nurturer becomes the destroyer, the griefs are endless. It just drove me deeper, to try not to turn my back on it.

While few of us will go through as dramatic a break as Susan did with her mother, the parent-child relationship simply cannot continue as it was during the first journey of our life. We change as we move from our thirties into our forties and our parents change as they move into their later years. Some older parents make the transition well, choosing to create new, creative relationships with their children—and some do not. Some adult children move into mid-life creatively, prepared to deal with their parents as adults—and some do not. Letting go of what was is not enough. We need to reconcile ourselves with those who in many ways matter the most to us. And if the other person is not responsive to reconciliation, we have to find ways to do this for ourselves. Susan chose to reconcile her relationship with her mother using the power of symbol.

> After she died I had the luxury to create a memorial service for her and to find some way in that very public, ritual occasion to speak the truth about how hard things had been, to find ways to thank everyone and to release people from the memories of the brokeness. Within a room filled with pain, we gave everyone a rose to offer as a symbol to say "may the beauty live on" with our other relationships. It was an immense relief and brought a sense of fulfillment to be an agent for healing after having been seen as "the enemy." It was the one gift I could give my mother that she couldn't refuse—a love for her that had been turned away for so long that I could finally express without her being able to thwart it. Rituals are so complementary to our powers of language. I'm a great champion of language but it fails us at certain points.

Susan's solution of creating a symbol to bring hope in the midst of hopelessness is a good strategy for anyone. Marilyn Melville counsels and leads workshops for people in mid-life. She confirms the importance of developing mid-life rituals as Susan did, to recognize times of letting go and of embracing what we wish either to be at peace with or to bring into being.

> We have rituals that we don't call rituals—like fortieth birthday celebrations. But when mid-life comes, people are in isolation and they often have no one to really share it. Ritual becomes a way to mark this time and acknowledge this transition because people are so encouraged when they see that others are going through what they're going through.

Marilyn invites people to bring symbols to her workshops but the symbols may be like dreams, and sometimes it takes someone the whole length of the workshop to discover the meaning of their symbol. We carry them with us without knowing what they truly mean. Every time I move house I discover that there are certain symbols—old letters, an old candle, a particular picture—that the rest of my family expects me to toss away as junk, but I can not. I have not tried to explain why these things are important to me but I know that they are. I carry them with me, and when I am able to articulate their meaning I will have identified symbols that are still important to me at mid-life.

Susan found meaning in the rose, a symbol of love and beauty that pointed to difficulty as well as kindness, that helped her to let go of dashed hopes for her relationship with her mother while giving her mother a final, uncompromised gift and signalling a way to build relationships from here.

*What good, new things are emerging for you as you let go of other things?*

The rose took on meaning because it was shared with others. Objects carry meaning when shared within significant relationships. The mid-life sense of isolation that Marilyn describes can be addressed only by making connections with others. A public act of letting go of the past to prepare for the future can bring healing to all who are involved. Perhaps fortieth birthday parties are more important than one might first think—especially if meaningful symbols are brought to the celebration!

Marilyn has another interesting take on this matter of letting go.

What I've learned about mid-life is that who you were before doesn't feel authentic and people sometimes want to throw out everything that went before and say, "*That* wasn't me—*this* is me!" But the challenge is to reconcile the different parts of yourself because often at mid-life they come into conflict. We want to dismiss that other person but in fact we're both people. The real challenge is to reconcile the past to the present.

Deciding that I'm no longer going to produce, consult, or teach because I am discovering my "artistic" side simply would not make any sense for me. Years of practice have given me ability and expertise, and working with these strengths brings a sense of accomplishment. And the work is still important work to me. However, I will let go of my need to only do what I feel I should or only what I am good at, so I can risk making some mistakes, move into new territory, and learn some new things. I want to build my repertoire without turning my back on who I have been and without falling into the trap of elastic living.

This need to reconcile the old with the new also has implications for relationships. What is happening to the stereotypical forty-year-old who dramatically discards a marriage and a staid lifestyle to buy a sports car and grab a new dance partner? To let go of the old and take on the new sometimes looks deceptively simple. But, without doing the work of reconciling the past to the present, people often find themselves in the same kind of circumstances they were trying to let go of. They may not have let go of anything truly significant—or taken on anything of comparable value.

While there is grief involved in relationships and possibilities that die, letting go is not all about sombre grieving or settling for less than we were before. In fact, a number of people spoke about the gains that result from the losses. A number of mid-life women, for example, spoke to me about their new and emerging self confidence.

Fredelle said,

When I was younger, I deferred to others, not trusting my own judgment on big issues. Now I simply make a decision. I trust my judgment and if people disagree with

me I can answer with confidence. It gives me a sense of
fulfillment that's in stark contrast to the image of middle-
aged women that popular magazines, videos, and television
programs put out. Their image is often of a woman who is
dissatisfied because her youth is behind her, who's margin-
alized because she's no longer sexually attractive. That's not
been my experience at all. I think in fact, that it's a relief not
to be treated primarily as a sexual target. That's not putting
down my sexuality but that I feel more in control.

In other words, it is a mid-life relief to claim one's strength and ability,
letting go of social pressures and expectations that have eaten away at self-
confidence.

Guru Raj said something very similar about what she decided to see
when she looked in her mid-life mirror.

I found forty to be a real turning point. For me, up 'til
then I had the feeling that "when I grow up, I'll be better
at this and that and this vice or that weakness will be
overcome." Suddenly I looked at myself and said "Wait a
minute—I am grown up—this is it!" If, in that moment, I
had said "What a mess!" then it would be downhill from
there. But, by God's grace, I looked and said "Hey, this is
pretty good'—not because there isn't anything wrong but
because of a sense of self acceptance. I'll work with my good
qualities and try to downplay the negative ones.

Guru Raj's spiritual perspective is rooted in being Sikh. She says, "My
doubts ended at mid-life. I suddenly realized that God's on my side."

Fredelle spoke as a Jewish woman, about a deepening appreciation
for—and openness to—the help and perspectives of others.

I've made a point in mid-life of being much more open
to other people's understandings. I don't feel I have to help
people understand the *correct* way of doing things but rather
I simply listen to them and go from there. I'm probably less
into "isms" than I was earlier in my life. I see the faith

journey for everyone as a personal journey fraught with difficulties and I don't think an "ism" is the answer or necessarily satisfying. For instance, liberalism doesn't answer questions any better than traditionalism does.

I feel more like a person who's trying things on for a fit with my understanding and my experience. For example, there are some ritual practices within Judaism which I'm not ready to practise but I haven't totally rejected them, whereas twenty years ago I think I would have had a speech about why nobody should do them.

I don't know anybody who hasn't experienced pain in their life. Even if I'm only looking at them from the outside, observing them at the other end of the streetcar where they look like they've got it all together, I'm sure that they've had a painful life experience. It's probably that insight more than any other that has helped me move away from the sin of envy and has made me more empathetic to other people. I wasn't so empathetic when I was younger. I tended to be more judgmental.

I was struck by what Fredelle and others described as letting go of hard and fast positions that were easier to proclaim in young adulthood. Another mid-life paradox appears to be that greater mid-life confidence can be gained while embracing a greater openness to those who are different from ourselves. Perhaps it was our earlier need to fit in and to know that we were with others like us that linked our self-confidence with "the correct position." If we did not have the confidence to stand alone we had to find and stake out our "camp." Now we have the option of claiming our security outside of a particular set of peer positions.

During our first journey of life we are also often filled with expectations for purity that we have come to know are hard to live up to! Life experience has introduced shades of grey and the potential for a gently growing openness to consider other ways. We can choose to be a little gentler with ourselves and with others.

As a young adult I had clear, strong views on everything from the best forms of world government to the healthiest breakfast food. (I'm still not prepared to say that forcing down daily brewer's yeast milkshakes didn't benefit my sons in utero!) But I took these positions with a degree of certainty and smugness that has melted away with the years. A competitive streak made me blind to my weaknesses—or at least reluctant to acknowledge them—even to myself. Experience has taught me that there are many approaches to any situation, many gracious ways in which another's sight can be brought to my blindness—and vice versa. I can now ask for help in seeing things another way, while feeling more confident than ever in who I am.

I suppose this highlights a potential mid-life danger as well. If we cannot find the grace to see shades of grey and let go of needing to be exclusively right, we will cling to our old ways and shatter along with them. The people with whom I spoke simply did not represent this kind of attitude.

A few years ago a Mennonite friend told me that his community did not prescribe a list of acceptable and unacceptable positions or activities for its members but instead encouraged people to do their own discernment based upon what would be good for their souls. That discernment, of course, includes reference to the faith community's teachings but it also encourages each person to do his or her own hard thinking. "What would be good for my soul?" is a question to which mid-lifers can bring their years of experience and learning about life's textures. Like Fredelle, we may reconsider positions we might have opposed when we were younger—if they are congruent with the wisdom and sense of life's complexity that we've gained with age.

*What helps you to discern what is good for your mid-life soul, as it lets go and opens up?*

It is unwise to generalize based upon a very limited number of conversations, but I find myself wondering if a growing confidence in mid-life women is matched by a dwindling confidence in mid-life men. Confidence has not appeared to come as easily to young women in my life as it has to young men. I suspect there are myriad reasons for this, including a complex interplay between how boys arrive in the world and how society builds up their confidence—or their need to appear confident.

Gerald reveals an underside to male confidence. He spoke to me as a deeply reflective Baha'i who is having difficulty letting go of ambitions that have not been fulfilled at the age of fifty. He has taught and written and done some television production and now he's been promoted into management.

> A few years ago I felt very productive and now I've been brought up short with the challenge of questions like "Who am I?" "Where can I make the best contribution?" and "What do I want to do with the rest of my life?" I'm at an age where you get pushed into management and I'm not sure I'm really good at it. I don't feel that I've accomplished everything I want to accomplish in terms of production, writing, and television.
>
> It's a spiritual challenge when you realize that your ego is tied up in producing things. The big challenge is to reduce the ego, to become submissive. It's a concept in the Christian church, in Judaism, is very important in Islam, and in our Baha'i religion too. So I say to myself, "Gerald, you're just not accepting the fact that you've got a big ego. Set it aside and be a teacher and mentor to others, help younger people to shine." But there's the feeling that if that's really true then I really am getting older and I've lost my chance. I've got to help myself understand the reality, to say "You're not going to write that book. Maybe you'll write an article." But that lowering of expectations is a really big challenge. I suspect it's about learning about spiritual reality.

Gerald speculates that much of his anxiety about having to let go of some of his unfulfilled goals is because he was brought up in a very competitive world where he always had to do well in sports and excel in school.

> I think that's really damaged us. I'm convinced that I'm a victim of that bad philosophy of competition. Instead of excelling at what I do best, I compare myself with others as I was always compared to them as a kid. It's so artificial and damaging. I'm secretly pleased that my son is not interested in competitive sports. I think men in particular have real

problems with this and suspect that they surface more as
men get into middle age.

A lot of men are lonely and dissatisfied because they were
socialized to measure themselves against certain yardsticks
so that by fifty, you would have written that book or accomplished that goal. It's very hard to realize you're not as good
as you thought you were.

When asked how he deals with this, Gerald immediately answered
"prayer" but went on to speculate that meditation was a more attractive,
yet difficult option.

I've found lately that I like to go off in the quiet. I think
that's why men like fishing. They're out there just kind of
meditating. I've been struck lately with how agreeable and
attractive it is and want to begin exploring it.

Gerald goes on to use an image that is in stark contrast to fishing. He
suggests that life up to this point is like a battleground, and perhaps this
is how many feel, men especially. What happens if you no longer feel up
to the fight?

There's a very wise saying about how there's a stage in life
when you have to be on the front line, and then there comes
a stage when you have to drift to the middle and coordinate
things. Then the stage comes when you have to go to the
back of the battleground and sit on the mountain and watch
the fight go on and just praise God and cheer on your
fellows.

Gerald is clearly struggling with whether it is time to move towards
praising God and cheering on others while unsure that he wants to leave
the battlefield.

Margaret Fisher Brillinger spoke at the beginning of this chapter
about elastic living, and about how we cannot add to and stretch out our
lives indefinitely. We may need to release some friendships "in love" as
my spiritual director says, and we may, indeed, need to release ourselves

and others from hard standards of judgment—again, in love. As a Christian, I see this mid-life call to let go of things we have held tightly, as an opportunity to experience God's grace. How else can we experience the depths of God's love unless we let go of our obsessions and fears in order to fall into the arms of that love?

Letting go of disappointments and grudges is part of letting go of our judgments and of releasing ourselves and others in love. The need for forgiveness flowed throughout these conversations as a steady theme and Al Evans, the psychologist and minister whom we met in the previous chapter, confirmed that it is a central piece of the mid-life spiritual experience.

He points out that we need to forgive ourselves as well as others. We have been players in a lot of relationships by this stage in life, and by the very nature of relationships, this means that we have hurt and have been hurt by people who are important to us. We carry old wounds, disappointments, and grudges and while we have probably grown and changed as we have moved through these relationships, now is the time for coming to terms with any required forgiveness, compassion, and justice.

Guru Raj argues that forgiveness is not only about forgiving others and ourselves. She thinks that it is really about forgiving God.

> The other person is also connected to God, so whatever's happening here has to do with God's plan. Forgiving someone is basically a giving of our gifts to them. When someone seems to be ruining our lives, we're not seeing what's really going on and that there's some kind of karmic contract between me and that other person which won't go away until we give each other gifts. God's plan is intricate and complicated, based upon souls giving each other gifts. We look at difficulties as if we're being punished but somewhere along the line we agreed on a soul level to meet this person in this life and either destroy one another by hate or liberate one other through love.
>
> I remember when my ex-husband owed me money which I deserved and I realized that pushing for that money would cause him more pain and that my contract with him

was about spiritual support. I let it go and suddenly started
to relate to him like a brother who still deserves my prayer
and not my blame. It was one of the most spiritual
experiences I've had. It opened up my heart and ability to
understand the nature of forgiveness. It's a middle-age thing
because I realized the relationship between God and my soul
is between me and God. I'm the only one who can open my
heart and I refuse to let anyone close it! I don't have time for
pettiness and for closing my heart anymore because there's
only so much time left for this part of the journey.

She goes on to talk about the time of her dad's death as a time for
learning about forgiveness.

I wanted to pray for his soul and realized that in order to
do that I had to forgive him. He was a worshipper of the
Virgin Mary, so I had to pray to her essence, to say "Here is
your son who's coming who you need to help" and I
couldn't add "even though he did this and that!" There's
such power in forgiving and allowing our love to heal.

Guru Raj's words remind me of my final days with my own father.
Dad had been one of the most friendly, outgoing people I have ever
known. To prove the point, a few days after his funeral, I went to my
parents' bank, to take care of something for my mother at the counter.
The teller noticed the last name on the cheque and asked if I was Dad's
daughter. When I told her about his death, tears came to her eyes. She
had only known him during the course of a couple of years, in occasional
conversations at the bank counter but she had to tell me what a
wonderful person he was.

The stroke that left Dad unable to speak seemed like the cruelest fate
of all. He was robbed of his ability to joke and visit with ease. His words
refused to be organized into sensible sentences but they kept coming.
Fortunately I could still usually tell by his cadence when the punchline
had arrived and I would laugh on cue, to his delight, though I had no
idea what I was laughing at.

During one hospital visit, quite suddenly in the midst of a stream of disconnected words, he said clearly, "Mardi, I'm sorry." I was taken aback. I had no idea what he was talking about but I knew in an instant that this was a God-given opportunity. It was a moment in which I could choose to be touched by grace or refuse to let our relationship change. I took a deep breath and went for it. I said "I forgive you." I let go of the rationalization that he might have been apologizing for some meaningless little thing.

The fact is, Dad had spent many years as an alcoholic. And even after his ten years of recovery, I still clung to built-up anger. In that moment I let go of my moral superiority. I will never know what the words meant to Dad but for me they were a turning point. Like Guru Raj, I felt the power in forgiving and in allowing myself to be healed. I pray that Dad felt healed too. I believe he did.

*Who and what do you need to forgive?*

Forgiveness is central to the mid-life spiritual journey, the ultimate opportunity to let go of all that holds us back from new life. We may need to let go of resentments towards a parent or spouse, a child or an employer, a friend who has turned away, or a community that doesn't seem to want us. If we pour our energy into holding onto judgments and resentments we'll have nothing left for beginning a new life, the second journey that will require all of the risking and openness we can muster.

So far, I have chosen to let go of three big mid-life grudges— sometimes it has involved physically reaching out to offer the other an embrace, to heal the wound. As I have let go of each grudge, it has let go of me. It no longer requires the worry or energy it once did. It is gone and I am free to move on.

Those whom we have met in this chapter might suggest that the first person we need to forgive is ourselves, to let go of expectations of perfection that we have not met, or inadequacies that can depress us. They would suggest that this is a time to look in the mirror and see what is good in ourselves and in others, so that we can reconcile ourselves with the past and become more compassionate.

And this is not a singular exercise. It requires symbolic actions with others, whether they be those we are forgiving or those who can help us work through our forgiving.

I have decided to gather and share with friends some of the symbols that represent what I need to let go of, in order to move more fully into the second journey of my life. These will be symbols related to my work, but also to my roles as daughter, parent, spouse, and friend. And as I do so, I will repeat lines from a prayer entitled "Loosen My Grip" in *Guerrillas of Grace* by Ted Loder:

> *Loosen my grip*
> *on my ways and words,*
> *on my fears and fretfulness*
> *that letting go*
> *into the depths of silence*
> *and my own uncharted longings,*
> *I may find myself held by you*
> *and linked anew to all life*
> *in this wild and wondrous world*
> *you love so much,*
> *so I may take to heart*
> *that you have taken me to heart.*

# 3
# The Personals

**"Time grants some of us, if we are very lucky, a travelling companion with whom to gather experience against its ravages."**

*Alberto Manguel*

*I* married when I was a very young adult—at the unripe age of almost twenty-one! It was an enormous leap of faith. I remember trying to explain to well-meaning naysayers that my deep desire was to create a home with this man. That desire had many more dimensions to it than youthful lust. I didn't know it then but I have come to learn that marriage has enabled us to come home to ourselves as well as to one another.

Doug and I came from diametrically opposed world views. He was a rationalist and deeply distrustful of things that could not logically be proven. Rationality was not so important to me as I saw the world through the eyes of a person who felt touched by God's irrational love and believed that what grew from that was all that really mattered.

Perhaps these deep differences caused us to be careful with our wedding vows. We did not promise to be faithful to one another *alone*. This was the early seventies, after all, and we bought into what I now see as the illusion that we might be faithful to one another without necessarily limiting ourselves to one another. Open marriage was attractive. We were young.

We are now in mid-life and after twenty-six years of marriage have a deeper understanding of faithfulness. I now know what I meant when I said I wanted to create a home with this man and it had nothing to do with place. We have created a safe, supportive relationship for each of us to venture from, to grow from, and to return to. And our personalities have developed with one another's support. I value my intellect more than I did twenty years ago and Doug now values his heart. One morning last spring I was startled to realize that we had, in some ways, traded places. Doug was taking time to admire the magnolia blossoms outside our bedroom window while I was preoccupied with what I needed to do to negotiate a big contract.

This should not have surprised me given all of the Jungian writing about how at mid-life our "inferior functions" or less-developed aspects of our personalities start tugging at the sweater sleeve of our souls, demanding our attention until we come to appreciate them. Such writing also emphasizes the importance of integrating opposites on the road to what Jung calls individuation, or becoming whole human beings.

Flora Litt provides spiritual companionship in ways that help people listen to God for themselves and also reflect upon how God has been with them throughout their life journeys. She has also studied the relationship between personality and spirituality. She talked with me about how the male energy or "Animus" in Jungian psychological terms typically emerges and develops for women in mid-life while men are at the same time developing their "Anima" or feminine side. The male task is often more difficult because the business scene still supports a notion that says: "Get out there and be productive." If that is supported and rewarded, it is often a tremendous challenge for men to find the other side. "If a man doesn't invite and allow for that growth, it can be explosive and that's what mid-life crisis is all about."

I am grateful that Doug felt drawn to smell the magnolias. God has apparently drawn us in a creative way to yearn for the other side of ourselves, to come closer to wholeness as we embrace both masculinity and femininity in our middle years. And these fundamental shifts profoundly affect our most intimate relationships.

*How have your closest relationships helped to shape your own mid-life journey?*

Jungian psychologists are particularly helpful to us in understanding how our personalities go through dramatic development at mid-life, working towards synthesis and wholeness. We are drawn towards integrating aspects of our personalities—some that have become well developed and others that are not so well-developed.

Whether we're single or attached, support from friends and loved ones can help us through these changes but understanding them for ourselves comes first. For Doug and me, our relationship has proved to be an incubator for the emergence of our fuller selves and it is only at mid-life that the nature of this evolution is becoming clear. To be in a relationship of acceptance, warts and all, provides a secure base and partnership from which to search further for meaning.

Margaret Fisher Brillinger observes that mid-life couples can provide one another with comfort and with challenge and that it's most often through their differences that partners help one another grow spiritually.

In Jungian terms, I am an extroverted intuitive with a personal preference to seek out one new experience after another. I enjoy dealing with all kinds of diverse projects and extensive personal contacts at the same time. Mid-life, however, is forcing me to face my limits and is attracting me to more private reflection with focus. I am no longer satisfied with breadth over depth. Until now I have also tended to be far more interested in the world of ideas than in the physical realities of the moment and I find myself shifting gears here as well. A good discussion has always been recreational for me but now I am discovering the joys of getting out of my head and into my body. Physical, down to earth activities like hiking and biking have introduced me to previously undeveloped avenues for living life to the fullest and feeling whole.

*What shifts in your own inclinations and desires are affecting your relationships?*

As I shift my attention from constant external activity to paying more attention to spiritual stillness, I find myself less interested in maintaining a large network of friends and more interested in nurturing a few, at a deeper level. Long, quiet conversation with a friend has become more satisfying than a series of short, energetic chats at a noisy party. In contrast, a more introverted mid-life friend recently described how she is becoming more drawn to and comfortable with extroverted activities like those party conversations.

A central mid-life question is "When I'm with this person, do I feel enriched and growing?" This does not mean that we are to pursue relationships only for ourselves, because it turns out that those in which we are needed can also become the most mutually enriching.

I mention my own experience as just one example of what numerous books demonstrate about how we tend to want to explore our "opposite inclinations" at this time in our lives. Books such as *Navigating Midlife* by Eleanor S. Corlett and Nancy B. Millner, demonstrate how each personality type seeks mid-life balance in its own peculiar way.

Achieving wholeness is a spiritual goal for just about everyone and mid-life presents unprecedented opportunities for getting closer to achieving it. We have an opportunity to appreciate and integrate more aspects of our own personality. In our relationships it means we are given the opportunity to understand and appreciate others' approaches as well, supporting them in their own evolution and celebrating their authentic selves as much as our own. In the previous chapter, Fredelle spoke about her mid-life openness to others' points of view. For me, Jesus' words to love one another as we love ourselves take on new meaning at this stage. I have a capacity to live those words in a way I never have had before.

First, I have come to a mid-life point of recognizing that I have lovable qualities. Second, I have become mature enough to celebrate that others' lovable qualities stand in contrast to my own.

As we change within ourselves, our relationships change as a consequence. When we are no longer interested in playing our part and reading our lines in one particular way, others in the scene may be disoriented, wondering what happens to their lines now! While this can be liberating for everyone eventually, it may also be threatening. This is one of the reasons why mid-life can be a time of great upheaval in relationships.

It is as if we have lived as pieces of a big, beautiful jigsaw puzzle and at mid-life someone decides to shake the pieces loose and challenge us to be part of creating a new and different picture. All the pieces get mixed up and need re-sorting to figure out their new relationships with one another. One of the consequences of my new choices is that I will likely lose contact with some of the people who have been important to me in the past—my piece may now be further away from theirs. Adjustments will be required but this does not diminish the value of what was before. In my case it has also meant that I have chosen to invest greater time in friendships that were not particularly close before.

Within my marriage it is no longer enough to carve out a little bit of time for one another in between heavy travel and work commitments. We have found it absolutely necessary to reserve unproductive time together, to walk and talk with greater depth. Like many mid-life couples, our children have matured to a stage where they no longer require the amount of immediate attention they once did, so time and energy that was pulled away from our marriage can now be returned to it.

The rewards can be deeply satisfying. But sometimes the need for personal growth and change can cause trauma.

Women or men who have stayed in unsatisfying relationships "for the sake of the children" may need to claim their mid-life courage to free one another in love when the relationship does not hold the capacity for growth.

Love affairs outside of marriage can, with hard work, push marriages in new directions. Margaret Fisher Brillinger observes that "an affair doesn't end a marriage. If affairs ended marriages we'd have a far higher divorce rate than we've got because the number of people who have affairs is huge. The couple has to decide what to do with it and it's a great opportunity for maturing if people work it through."

There may be as many reasons for mid-life affairs as there are people having them. But as Fisher Brillinger says, if you've lived with someone for many years a lot of marriage becomes humdrum, and of course, kids storm into a couples' life, hang around for twenty years or so, and then leave, sometimes leaving their parents' relationship in shambles. It takes effort to get to know one another again and start a whole new life together.

I have been struck by the deep ambivalence and confusion that people express, during mid-life retreats, about their primary sexual relationships. One minute participants talk about their desire and strategies for rekindling youthful passion and the next they are saying that all they want is to "snuggle without pressure." Anxiety about partner expectations seems to be equally distributed between women and men. At the end of the day, intimacy and acceptance seem to emerge as their greatest desire with the hope that fun and excitement will continue to season the journey.

*What relationships do you need to "release in love" and what relationships do you want to invest or reinvest in?*

Starting over with someone new can, of course, look a lot easier.

A woman whom we will call Mary spoke to me about her own mid-life discoveries through the experience of an affair. She and her husband started dating in their last year of high school and married two years later. They had their children early on and she began her teaching career in her late thirties. A few years later, in her early days of mid-life she started to read feminist writing and became very angry. Her anger interfered with their marriage. When her husband believed that she was angry with him personally, he found a woman friend with whom he could talk more easily.

Mary became terribly jealous and, apart from having her career back, this was a very unhappy time. She and her husband grew further apart and then she met a younger man. Unlike her husband's new relationship, Mary's developed into a passionate love affair.

This happened ten years ago; she was forty-one. Her lover was a good looking, younger man. At first she was flattered that he had thought she was younger, and then that her true age did not matter to him once he knew it. She believed she could continue the relationship without ending her marriage.

Before long Mary realized that her marriage was in danger and decided that she did not want to lose it. She ended the affair with great difficulty and talked with her husband about what had happened. They then began the hard work of rebuilding their relationship with the help of counselling.

She remembers the counsellor saying that it is more likely the marriage will survive when the man has had the affair than when the woman has. I don't know whether this means women are more forgiving than men, but Mary is deeply grateful that her husband was willing to move with her through pain and anguish.

Faith struggles were clearly in the mix:

> I think I am a good Christian woman and the more Christian women I meet I find there are all kinds of things going on. While I regret the affair, maybe it had to happen for us to get a grip and decide whether we really wanted our marriage or not. Maybe our marriage would have gotten more and more uncommunicative.
>
> We're much more conscious of our relationship now than when we were younger and took it for granted. Sex is now more like I think most women like it, making love when I

feel like it. It's wonderful when you feel a person loves you enough to wait for the right moment for you. Sex for both of us is a very spiritual, beautiful thing and we nurture it in our fifties by being proud of our bodies and enjoying them and not being afraid to say what we want. Last week we were near a beach and I said I'd really like to make love on the beach and we did. It's important to say "I can still do this" at this age. The closeness in which we can share all of our thoughts and feelings is part of our spirituality.

I found it remarkable that Mary not only told her husband about her affair but she also told her mother who, as a result, opened up about difficult times with her dad. Her mom's nervous breakdown at the age of fifty came into clearer focus. Mary's daughters also know about their parents' difficulties, which may help them gain perspective when they reach this stage.

Mid-life honesty injected new energy into all of these relationships. Without such honest struggle these relationships might very well have died in spirit.

Paul came into mid-life as a gay man who had so rigidly controlled himself during the first half of his life that there was little space for honesty about his sexual orientation, let alone a place for sex itself. He had known that he was gay from the time he was a teenager but he went through the motions of dating girls so that he would not lose his friends. He was an accomplished young man who became a respected child care worker and ordained minister. But the fears about what might happen if anyone found out who he really was became too great. It was not a fear that he would be discovered in any kind of inappropriate behaviour. But during his late thirties he had begun to open the closet door just enough to tell a few people. He knew it was just a matter of time before word got around. The work that he loved and on which his very livelihood depended would be threatened. The burden of his fear grew too heavy as he approached forty. He suffered burnout.

I had to let go of old friendships which wanted to keep me in fear and keep me in the closet. I let go of my vocation and my security. When I left the church it wasn't as if I had someplace to go but I had to get out from under the fear. I felt like the fear was suffocating me and killing my soul. I was afraid that I was going to die spiritually and maybe physically because yes, I had thoughts of suicide when I was depressed.

I needed to find a healthy way to live with who I was created to be. I had hoped to find acceptance in the church and maybe that's why the church appealed to me, but it didn't provide me with that as a gay man.

A deep desire for integrity was a key part of this. I needed to find a place where I could be true to who I was. When I decided to be out, not to live with lies or fear anymore, I was prepared to sweep floors if that was the only job I could get. And I had to overcome my own internalized homophobia. I didn't know how to be gay because I'd put such restrictive boundaries around myself—no sex, no partner, fear of AIDS, and all kinds of other fears.

Paul left a small town to live in the city. He found himself at home in a gay neighbourhood and found work for which he was ideally suited. He provides counselling and consultation within a residential program for high-risk teenagers who may have spent time on the street, left intolerable home situations, or may be in treatment or rehabilitation, sometimes as young offenders. The freedom he now feels to be honest with himself and others has enabled him to help younger people as they begin their own life journeys towards self-acceptance.

I never knew I could be so happy, that I could be happy being me, and that my life could be so whole. I look at the work I'm doing and see really tangible results for these kids. When I sit with some of these kids, I know I'm the only person in their life who they can talk to honestly and be respected for who they are. I know that's a gift and I know that I'm making a difference in finding ways to better serve these kids. When I began to come out to some of my colleagues, my supervisor said, "I'm glad you've come out because now you can use all of your gifts on the job."

The mid-life freedom to see ourselves clearly, without being blinded by what the world sees, offers the possibility of turning what we thought were liabilities into gifts. Paul describes how at forty-two he feels settled for the first time in his life. The fact that he has taken a full-time, permanent position is in itself a new venture. For years before, he had chosen to work on short-term assignments to protect himself from becoming too attached or too well-known, out of his fear that if people really knew him and he got too attached to them, it would be too painful.

During the first half of his life Paul owned few possessions and travelled the world in between job assignments. Now he has begun to nest. He has bought a condominium, has nice furniture and plants and even a cat. Most people "settle down" in these ways during the first part of their lives and may be letting go of these patterns in mid-life. While it may appear that Paul is living his life in reverse, he is really doing the same thing by letting go of first journey patterns.

> I'm starting over because I've found my place. I'm now with my own people. A white friend who adopted a black child told me that when the child was sixteen or seventeen he was exposed to black culture and felt that he had discovered his own people. That relates to my discovery. I'm finally living out my teenage years. I'm dating now and I go dancing two or three times a weekend. After a year and a half of living like a seventeen-year old, I'm now feeling another shift. I've had my fun and now I'm really hoping to meet someone I can date regularly with intimacy.

Like other mid-lifers Paul spent the first part of his life accommodating himself to the external world that, in his case, required hiding his true self. He was a very mature young man without the opportunity to play that straight teens and young adults had. As with other mid-lifers, his early forties have made him yearn for and seek integrity, which in his case means doing some things he did not have a chance to do earlier in life.

To family and long-time friends, Paul's mid-life maturation may appear to be immaturity. "As a kid I was a good boy. I would sit quietly and play nicely and as I became a teen, I felt that my connection was tenuous—if they really knew, I wouldn't be accepted here." He now wonders how people who are important to him may react to less socially accepted behaviour, but that is no longer enough to control him.

Paul has always placed high value on his spiritual life. This was, no doubt, nurtured by Christian parents, one of whom was an ordained minister like himself. Working with high-risk teenagers has continued to remind him of the importance of spiritual discipline. He describes these disciplines as ways to get his mind and body in sync in order to become centred and sort out what he is not going to worry about.

> Living this settled lifestyle is different from my earlier life
> of living on the edge where I had to rely on my creator
> every day. I used to have a sharp sense of connection with
> my creator when I was travelling into new places and living
> without knowing what might happen next. Now my
> spiritual life has more of a rhythm than a sense of edge.

Paul says that the challenge now is to keep his faith alive while focusing on being "centred, grounded, and balanced." It was a spiritual retreat with other gay men where Paul felt safe to talk about and understand his journey. He regularly returns to this network and to others that he has discovered in his new life.

Mary also spoke about the importance of this kind of support. Her women's spirituality group has provided a close, safe community in which middle-aged women share their lives with one another. "It's been a meaningful way for me to think about issues in life and to worship. I see worship as a very social activity and being with these people allows me to gain inner strength as we read and talk about books for example."

Navigating the mid-life spiritual journey is easier with the help of other mid-life travellers. While spiritual practices are frequently thought to be private, Paul and Mary and others have made it clear that their investment in support groups represents an equally important spiritual practice.

But not everyone makes their way within a community of faith. Debbie is one who makes her own way spiritually. Debbie's work involves training social workers in how to investigate child and family abuse. She is forty-two and her husband is fifty-two so her husband began his mid-life transition before she began hers.

My husband had become self-employed and was feeling that he wanted to move out of the city to be more in touch with nature. He started talking about selling everything, buying a boat, and sailing. I was very resistant. I was bent on having a purpose in my life and didn't see how living on a boat would give me a sense of purpose. So we talked about it for a couple of years to try to accommodate what he wanted to do and what I wanted to do.

I was in a doctoral program and I decided to study what happens within couples when one partner initiates a significant lifestyle change.

Debbie and her husband eventually made a significant change themselves, which has caused her to reassess what purpose itself is all about. They now live outside the city and spend considerable chunks of the year sailing, balanced by chunks of work time. Now in mid-life herself, she reports that the change has helped her become a more balanced person.

Changing their lifestyle was a result of negotiation. She cites the book, *Getting the Love You Need*, which helped them work towards understanding what the other person wants and focusing on that without becoming martyrs. She found this philosophy, in which each person focuses upon the other's need, to make sense both philosophically and practically.

I pointed out that this philosophy reminded me very much of instructions given by Jesus and other spiritual leaders throughout history. She agreed but explained that so far, she's had an aversion to organized religion.

In my younger years I didn't have time for the spiritual piece and now I've come to understand it as essential to self-actualization. Most of my work is with aboriginal people, which has touched me spiritually more than anything else in my life. Their holistic belief system attracts me as a way to find wellness at work and at play. When I choose projects, I prefer working with Native people because they tend to put on less of a facade and I'm drawn to that. They've taught me to stop asking questions; to slow down, watch, and listen and take in what's going on around me. I didn't appreciate that message [about slowing down] when I was younger. I remember, for example, watching people do Tai Chi when I was twenty-seven and thinking—"I can't do that—it's too slow." I chose power walks or climbed onto the treadmill.

Within the last couple of years Debbie has begun to think about notions such as God's work and what's involved in doing God's work.

A couple of years ago I had a split-second realization of what this notion of doing God's work means. To me, it means helping people to see that the world really is a wonderful, wonderful place so things like taking a pie to my neighbour or offering up my first class seat on the plane became things I wanted to do. I feel driven to helping people see the world as a beautiful place and I call that God's work! If we each took that responsibility and did a little piece, we'd be less cynical and less angry.

Perhaps it takes at least a few decades of living to come to believe what Debbie is saying, and many of my mid-lifers seemed surprised and delighted with such discoveries. Countless words from the world's religious traditions have instructed us to care for the other as a way to find peace, but mid-life seems to give us our best shot at trusting the truth of those words. Experience has taught us that trying to get the most out of every relationship does not bring peace any more than trying to get the most out of every work situation. At mid-life we may finally be ready to gently release the ego and take hold of the spirit just enough to see what happens when we focus on giving.

*Who longs for the benefit of your mature, mid-life care?*

This is, of course, tricky territory if we are dealing with relationships that have been unjust or abusive. Flora said: "Some have allowed themselves to be used and abused and a lot of women in mid-life are saying "I won't have that anymore.""

An awareness that life is going to end often prompts reassessment of how well we can live our lives within the relationships we are in. Flora goes on to speak to what she believes mid-life men and women desire in relationships:

> Men and women both want to be able to be who they are—to have a sense of being known, loved, and accepted without having to pretend, and to share some of the same goals in life. I think it's connected with the search for meaning and the fulfillment of basic needs. We want to know "What is my life all about and who is journeying with me?" Whether it's a spouse or friends we want partnership on the journey. I think it's a time when we know we need each other and the older we get the more we know we're going to need each other.

I explored the question of whether there are differences in the ways in which mid-life women and men approach relationships, with people like mid-life counsellor Marilyn Melville. Here's what she had to say:

> I'm surprised by how similar the issues for men and women are. One of the issues is loneliness which I think is especially true for men, partly because women are more accustomed to building relationships.
>
> I hear a lot of women express disappointment in their relationships and marriages. They're having difficulty reconciling what they had hoped for in the relationship with how it is. Another difference I think may be that there's a more cynical response to mid-life in men, and more depression in women.

Marilyn believes that while depression isn't something anyone wants to experience, it can lead to the rediscovery of a spiritual life. She tells the story of a woman who came to realize the presence of God in her depression and Marilyn went on to say "This wasn't dissimilar to my own experience. It was one of the most difficult periods of my life but I connected up to myself." Connecting with ourselves is part of feeling connected to God.

Depression is a complex matter and often arose in my conversations about mid-life, especially with women. While it may be triggered by any aspect of life including our relationship with our work or with physical changes, it comes into painful profile within close relationships. It will confuse and frustrate those who love us the most but the potential for new insight seems to be proportional to the pain.

A friend who recently suffered from clinical depression reported that one of the most effective prescriptions she received was from a doctor who told her to do something every day that would give her pleasure. Sometimes she chose a bubble bath, sometimes it was reading for enjoyment, or something else. On the surface this may appear to be a frivolous prescription, but she needed to nurture play in order to balance her work and to rediscover joy. What is play for her is not necessarily play for me. Each of us needs to search our soul and experiment with balance. There is potential for crisis when our lives become so unbalanced, yet even the crisis offers an opportunity for discovery. It seems to me that our western spiritual teachings focus far more on the value of work than play, so we often need to take a fresh look for spiritual teaching to meet our need for balance and wholeness.

Our relationships improve when we become clearer about how to take care of our own souls because then we can be clearer with others about what we need from and offer to them. When Flora Litt reflected upon Marilyn Melville's words about men's loneliness and women's dissatisfaction she reminded me that mid-life leads to questioning. Some of these questions may be: "What did the woman long for that she didn't find in the relationship?" "How has she allowed her own expectations to mature?" "Is what she longed for still there to find?" "What is mid-life impotence saying about a man's sense of identity?" "What imbalances and stresses are leading to loneliness?"

The questions at mid-life just keep coming and offer us a real opportunity for staying spiritually alive. It is important for us to nurture relationships in which we can work safely with our own questions.

It was striking in this regard how often mid-lifers told me about a newly deepening sense of appreciation for family and home. I began this chapter by describing my desire to make a home with Doug. I used those words when I was younger without fully knowing what they meant. I know now and my experience is clearly not unusual.

Angelos' story is interesting as a glimpse into this mid-life phenomenon. He describes his carefree young adulthood during which he enjoyed good times:

> When I was younger I didn't take on a sense of responsibility. I was free to do what I wanted, to spend what I wanted. I worked at any early age to support myself through school and was sharing a business which gave me a lot of money, relatively speaking, to the point where I could put myself through school and buy a car...I didn't have to plan for things.

He describes mid-life as a time when his sense of joy and responsibility for his family relationships has flourished and deepened in response to a crisis in his child's health. Angelos has a career in solid waste management, so his world view is practical and scientific.

> My focus now is my family. My mom is a very religious person but when I was younger I would go to church only on special occasions. When I met my wife she also came from a strong religious family. She's Roman Catholic and I was Greek Orthodox.
>
> As a scientist, I have my religious doubts, but as I've gotten older I've begun to think that this is an important component of life and I've been asking if I've lived my life appropriately. For me, church is primarily important as a family thing and we go almost every Sunday now.
>
> Church became very important to us when my son had cancer and he lost one of his eyes. We took him for the priest to bless before he went in for some surgery and things went very well. The priest who blessed my son died of cancer about three months later. It almost seemed like the priest took the illness from my son into himself. I know it doesn't make any sense at all but it feels like maybe this priest sacrificed his life and, ever since, things have unfolded in a good way for us. Maybe it's far-fetched but that priest will stay in our minds forever. If that had happened when I was younger I wouldn't have made that association. Our son

now lives as normal a life as possible with one eye.

My wife and I are much closer now. In some cases the strain of this kind of thing causes a break-up but it has strengthened our relationship. We talk more than we did when we were younger and about things that matter more.

The fact that Angelos is entertaining such unscientific thoughts about healing and sacrifice seemed a bit surprising even to him. He made it clear that he never would have considered such ideas before mid-life, but now he is contemplating mystery, and his family relationships are helping him do this.

Flora Litt's words relate to many aspects of mid-life including how we choose, begin, nurture, and end relationships during this stage of life.

There's a real longing in middle life to be real, to have integrity. Mid-life is a coming home to oneself, to who we really are, dropping masks and roles even to ourselves, which is where it has to happen first. I believe that each one of us comes here with work to do, with gifts to use for the sake of the world, with lessons to polish if not learn. Mid-life is a time when we realize how precious life itself is. It's a time when friends are dropping with cancer, when we're saying good-bye to parents and other older relatives, and we realize that we're not going to be here forever. You become very aware that every day is a precious gift and the question arises "How am I going to use it?"

*How are you coming home to yourself, and to those who are important to you?*

Doug and I chose to celebrate our twenty-fifth wedding anniversary by going on an eight-day hike along part of the Cornwall path in southwest England, hugging the northern Atlantic shoreline as we went. It was a choice that reflected a number of newly emerging mid-life commitments: living into a balance between our preoccupation with thoughts and ideas and the experience of seeing, touching, smelling, and tasting the beauty of the earth; living into a balance of time spent in work and in play; living into a balance between commitments made to others and commitments made to one another.

Yes, we filled our lungs with sea air, rejoiced in the distance covered with every sore muscle and blister, savoured the tastes of every bit of food and drink, and simply delighted in our far-from-young bodies. Our thoughts and ideas seemed as lively as ever in the midst of this sensual explosion. Much of our thinking seemed to parallel the path itself. We have been on a journey together, bringing one another home, time and time again. The distance has been long and we know that our earthly journey will not go on forever. Until it ends we will help one another over the rough spots as we have in different ways at other times, we will point to things that might otherwise be missed, encourage the other when the cliff looks like too much to tackle, and simply care for one another.

# 4
# *Cold Wars and Crumbling Walls*

**"You couldn't exorcise the past either by returning to it or by running away. You couldn't resolve to put it out of your mind and memory, because it was part of mind and memory. You couldn't reject it, because it had made you what you were. It had to be remembered, thought about, accepted, perhaps even given thanks for..."**

P. D. James, A Certain Justice

My father's death brought my life into clearer focus. Until then I had given little thought to the deeply personal ways in which life flows from one generation to the next. So much of our young adult lives seem devoted to separating ourselves from our parents in order to make what we think of as our independent way. But when Dad died I was overwhelmed with the pain of a severed connection.

In that moment, as I tried to match coherent words to feelings, my children expressed the pain in ways that brought light to those deep generational connections. From the moment I told our then ten-year-old son about his grandad's death, he had a stomach ache that lasted for days. When our minister visited, he began by asking "You know that pain you feel in your stomach?" (We hadn't said anything about stomach pain.) The minister described how eastern traditions believe that energy flows through us in relationships like those with our parents and grandparents, and we feel pain in the earthly severing of that relationship. The physical place of that connection is just below the navel. My son's pain provided evidence of this.

Dad's death was a drastic wake-up call to understand my connections with my parents and grandparents and it gave me an opportunity to think about my place in the middle, with those before me and those coming behind. It also alerted me to seeing that part of one's mid-life work is preparation for the end and for being the elder generation.

During my first mid-life session with my spiritual director, she suggested that I reflect upon Isaiah 51:1 "Listen to me, you that pursue righteousness, you that seek the Lord. Look to the rock from which you were hewn, and to the quarry from which you were dug." She was offering an avenue by which I could begin to reconcile myself with my own family history. As earlier chapters have shown, mid-lifers seek integrity. Such integrity relies upon the integration of all aspects of our experience, including our core experiences of our original family.

*What do you see in the rock from which you were hewn and the quarry from which you were dug?*

As I told her about my quarry—the lives of my grandparents and parents—I was filled with unprecedented appreciation and new-found sympathy for them, from my mid-life perspective. I heard myself telling her "Dad loved us very much." She stopped me abruptly and told me to repeat this sentence in the present tense. I obeyed and said "Dad loves us very much."

This helped me to realize that Dad's love was not gone. Nothing in this world is completely lost. It simply changes form. Dad's love lives and in this way, he lives. I decided to look up a letter that a wise friend had written to me when my Dad died and his words made new sense. John wrote about his own father's death, five years earlier, as a way to comfort me:

> At first when my father died, all I could feel was the gaping emptiness that his sudden disappearance left me. I felt like a black, aching hole that would never be filled.
>
> But as I got beyond the original shock and horror of it, I found that, in fact, my father hadn't really left me. He came to me after in dreams, each time assuring me that although he really was dead, he was still with me. And he came to me in my meditations in the form of the raven who never judged, but always supported and who actually carried me

upon his back to the places I needed to go.

And gradually I came to understand that he is with me. He lives in my memories, in words and phrases of his that I find myself repeating, in the way I hold an axe or paddle a canoe, in the joy I take in telling jokes and stories, in my empathy with Native people, in my compassion for others and in many, many other ways too numerous to count. His spirit broods over my life still, continuing to offer unconditional love and support as only a parent can.

And even though I still miss his actual physical presence, I know too, that he has gone so that I may continue in my own growth, so that I may more completely become the husband, the father, the writer, the adult male I am meant to be.

In a way, I see now, my father's death was his final gift to me, a letting go that frees me to become, in a way, more fully his son and more fully myself.

The death of a parent makes it impossible to hide from the spiritual challenges of mid-life. And whether it is through parental death or illness, the birth of our grandchildren, or something less dramatic, our mid-life souls seem destined to consider our place in the continuity of life. We are doing this, of course, while our own children are breaking away from us to make their own ways in the world. We are faced with needs for acceptance and reconciliation on all sides.

Cold, intergenerational wars may continue to be fought but we are given an unprecedented opportunity, with the wisdom of mid-life perspective and maturity, to reach out and break down the walls. No matter how high or how thick the walls appear, we must try to shatter them, for only in this way can we be reconciled with our own stories and our own lives and spirits. Sometimes our attempts are not warmly received, as illustrated by Susan's story in relation to her mother in the chapter on Letting Go. Recall that Susan did not let her mother's rejection stop her. She did what she needed in order to make peace with her mother in a way that her mother was not, ultimately, able to refuse. Susan's gift to her mother turned out to also be a gift to herself and her own soul.

Margaret Fisher Brillinger provides perspective both as a counsellor and as someone in the middle generation. She talks about how, on the one hand, our children are breaking away and, on the other hand, we are watching our parents grow old. The middle is an emotionally charged place to be.

> My parents are the only people who've always been in my life. They're the only people who've been there from the beginning so there's continuity. I never adjust to seeing them bent over, unable to do things they used to do and, whenever I recognize this, a shock wave goes through me. In my deep, emotional memory, they're energetic, vibrant, and active. Last week I walked in to visit and saw a little old lady with a cardigan buttoned up with mismatched buttons and holes. I realized that my mother is a little old lady.

Those who have cared for us in so many ways are now moving closer to needing our care. While the fulcrum point for physical care may shift from one side towards the other, shifts in spiritual care may not be so predictable. In fact, elders frequently demonstrate many spiritual gifts such as how to grow old with grace. We can receive lessons for aging as we watch and learn from what we want to emulate—or from what we may want to do differently. Margaret describes her parents as instructors in aging.

> As I watch my parents deal gracefully as bright minds with failing bodies, they're providing me with a rehearsal. I realize that this is the closest teaching I have before I get there myself so I'd better find out all that I can when I'm with them. Sometimes we joke about it and sometimes we cry. We've had to learn how to do that because in my family we don't talk about these personal, up-close things.

Psychologist Al Evans argues that being in between the generations before and after us is such a fundamental factor of the mid-life experience that people in their seventies can still think of themselves as mid-lifers if they are still looking out for their parents.

Being in the middle also puts us in an ideal position to help younger and older generations learn from one another. Margaret has had this experience.

> I find that I'm the interpreter across the generations,
> from my position within the inside of the sandwich. None
> of my children follow the mould. They're not married, they
> keep changing jobs and moving around and they travel to
> all kinds of interesting places. My parents were from a
> generation shaped by the depression so laying a groundwork
> for security with marriage and a job and saving to buy a
> bungalow were very important. But both my kids and
> parents share values that they don't immediately see in one
> another. My parents, for instance, would never waste a thing
> because experience taught them that you don't know if
> there's going to be anything there for you tomorrow. My
> kids don't waste anything because they have a deep concern
> for the planet. I can explain to my parents why one of my
> kids is working on a educational farm in California, in
> religious terms and language that make sense to them, and
> in a way that they can accept. I know the language of both
> so can interpret both ways, to help them see how underlying
> values cut across the generations.

Interest in working on family trees comes out of this orientation. At mid-life we realize the need to reconcile ourselves with the past, not just for ourselves but also for who is coming after us. As Margaret suggests, we are in the position that gives us a view backwards and a view forwards with a perspective on both past and future that brings some responsibility with it.

In fact, the middle is by definition a place in between. We are in between the generation from which we have come and the generation coming after us.

I had found my mother's interest in our genealogy rather precious during the first part of my life journey. It held no particular interest for me. Whenever she discovered a delicious tidbit about an ancestor's foibles or special talents, she would muse upon how that inclination or trait had turned up in later generations. I now find myself becoming interested.

My experience resonates with what I have heard others describe as a growing mid-life appreciation and acceptance of those from whom we came.

I was struck by a recent newspaper article in which a forty-five-year
old woman wrote about meeting someone who had known her mother,
who had died when the writer was sixteen months old. Since the writer's
father had also died when she was very young, she had had little
opportunity to learn about her parents. Now that she was a mid-life
mother herself, the yearning to know about them was almost painful.
Hearing from this older woman about what her mother and father had
been like and how they had loved one another gave her, for the first time,
a sense of where she had come from and what she was still a part of. She
described it as a wonderful, generous gift. She needed to gain a
perspective on the generation before her in order to be at peace within
her own mid-life soul.

Fredelle, who was introduced in an earlier chapter, told me that mid-
life was when she stopped trying to change her parents.

> I no longer get into quarrels with them about ideas I
> don't agree with. And since my mother's memory is failing
> she asks the same question six or seven times. I just answer
> the question again and again and I don't think I used to do
> that. I used to argue with her—about her shopping habits
> for example, and I don't do that anymore.
>
> My parents don't have to try to shape me or raise me
> anymore either. I'm delighted that they're happy to be with
> me, that they value my companionship. I feel like a beloved
> child.

When so much of life's first journey is shaped by intergenerational
conflict and struggle, the acceptance made possible in mid-life can bring
welcome relief to both mid-lifers and their parents.

Mary, whom we also met in an earlier chapter, tells a similar story:

> My mother and I have come to the stage where we can
> be friends and that was a mid-life transition for me. It
> happened when my mother reached the stage where she was
> no longer able to be totally independent. Before that, we

had often struggled in our relationship. I remember having to often say: "Mom, I'm an adult now—I'm thirtysomething or fortysomething." For a long time it was hard for her to respect our differences and I think I just gave up arguing with her. But now she respects that I have my own opinions on things.

My mom is a very fundamentalist Christian and that's what I grew up in. I have great respect for her beliefs and they were a great source of strength for my parents when they came to Canada from Holland. But, in my opinion, the church [transplanted to] Canada got stuck, so for me it became unfulfilling.

My mother now sees that I'm a good person, and while I let her know what I believe, I will not get caught in a web of argument. My earlier concern was to get to a place where I felt my mother respected me. Now I'm also more confident about that and about my own faith.

Perhaps the prospect of mutual respect can best be fulfilled when children become middle aged, because both parent and child are now mature adults. Each can receive the kind of respect they have longed for from one another, even when it may have been impossible earlier.

Maturity is one of the gifts of aging—and so is vulnerability. Mary found that it was her father's physical weakness that made a stronger relationship possible.

My father was a good man but you couldn't really have a conversation with him because he didn't listen. But as he got older and got cancer, he was careful to tell me that he loved me. He said he realized that he'd made a lot of mistakes in his relationship with my mother, so he became vulnerable in that state and a lot happened between us. My sister and I took time off work to be with him when he was dying. It was very difficult but I'm grateful now that I did it.

Growing vulnerability in those who are older than us, as well as the vulnerability that is growing within our own souls, provides a new opportunity for healing relationships with parents and other older relatives.

Beth told me about how her relationship with her parents has changed through the shifting balance of caregiving. This is a basic ingredient of what has been commonly described as the sandwich generation. We find ourselves as the filling in the middle, holding things together, as we provide care for those who are younger and for those who are older at the same time. Beth's father had already suffered several strokes before we spoke.

> I kiss and hug my father now whenever I see him. I didn't do that before—we never even kissed at Christmas in my family—and he's very responsive to it. Yesterday, when he was in emergency, he held my hand and just wouldn't let go. My mother would bristle at that kind of public show of affection, but now I don't care if she bristles or not and I want her to know that she can loosen up too.

Beth is not only taking the initiative to give care that has not been needed this way before, but she is demonstrating enough mid-life confidence to give it in different ways from how she received care from her parents.

The experience of watching our parents' generation grow old tells us that they will not always be there for us. A sense of urgency comes from a realization that our parents will be gone and we are going to be "it"—"the last line in the battle" as Hugh said to me. He went on to say

> Sometimes that feels very lonely and very desolate. When we were younger and having struggles with our work or with kids or needed a loan, Mom and Dad were usually there and you had a sense of security that there was somebody in the world for you, who would stand by you no matter what.

Once we accept that our parents will not be physically present with us forever, we are more apt to re-examine how we are spending this finite time with them.

I feel a greater need than before, to spend time with older relatives. I no longer take opportunities to visit as lightly as I used to, even though my life is still very demanding and it is hard to find the time. I am also beginning to try to say and do things that need to be said and done before it is too late.

*How is increasing vulnerability in yourself and in the generation before you creating new intergenerational opportunities?*

A few years ago my in-laws needed a driver to bring them home from their southern vacation. A minor injury made them feel insecure about tackling the three-day journey on their own. I was privileged to be the family member who could respond. Three days gave us the chance to get to know one another as we had not before, to challenge one another, to get on one another's nerves, to laugh with and at one another. Our relationship was improved by the sheer gift of intense time on our own.

Making time for siblings is also more attractive than it once was. These people with whom we share a family story have, like us, been busy with their own first journeys but there seems to be a mid-life desire to come together and get to know one another as adults for the first time.

When I reflect upon the quarry from which I was hewn, I realize that there are many things for which I have not said "thank you" that were real gifts to me. I was not able to recognize—let alone acknowledge these—during the first part of my journey.

Last summer I made sure that I had some time with my aunt so that I could tell her what had come from my reflections: she and my mother together provided me with wonderful role modelling. My mother focused her early adulthood upon raising her children; my aunt focused upon a successful career. Together they reflected the joys and sorrows of each choice and they showed me how such choices could be well lived.

I had planned to speak with my aunt alone but it turned out that my younger son was with me for that visit. I accepted that as an unexpected blessing. He saw and heard me expressing intimate gratitude to the generation before me. I live in hope that he may some day have reason to do the same!

Esta is almost sixty years old. She was forty-eight when her mother became very ill with a preventable illness. She has had to deal with related guilt and a shattered naïveté about life when dear ones have to deal with serious illness.

You think more deeply in mid-life about good, evil, and justice—looking for deeper meaning. All of the self-help stuff is obviously so shallow. I know from experience that there aren't easy answers.

I know I'm in mid-life because I've grown up. I've had to do more and look after others more. When you're the one supervising the family events, you can see the generational shifts and changes. Since my parents are no longer living, I now supervise these events. We just shared the [Jewish Passover] Seder with my grandchildren and there was a real sense of continuity, which pulls me through a lot.

I think of myself as the carrier of the tradition and the faith.

The implications of Esta's comments are profound—not only for ourselves but for those who follow us. It is time to take seriously our responsibility for carrying, interpreting, and giving leadership to expressions of our faith and hope. This will evolve into a central responsibility as elders in later years. So it is time now to start thinking about what our lives themselves are teaching.

While life remains busy, the time and energy freed from the many physical tasks of early parenting can be invested into the spiritual tasks of parenting (not that spiritual parenting did not inevitably begin earlier!). Even if it is only taking part in regular worship, contributing to a community of faith, and giving voice to our beliefs and commitments at special family gatherings such as the Seder, from our mid-life perspective we know that our actions will not be lost on younger ones who are watching and listening, even when they appear disinterested!

*In what ways do you see yourself moving into the role of elder?*

Our spiritual commitments no longer need to be presented as arguments or "positions" as we may have felt earlier in our lives. We may find it impossible to restrain ourselves from giving the next generation advice about job or relationship choices, but faith commitments are more fully about who we are at the middle of our lives. They are not so much about telling others what they should be. For one thing this is because we are more confident in our faith. For another, our own maturity and fatigue from the "shoulds" can enable us to be more gentle and less prescriptive about spirituality than we may have been during our first journey. Our own growing integrity holds the greatest potential for revealing and pointing to spiritual truth.

Nina is a university instructor, teaching in the areas of sociology of health and illness, minority group relations, and aging. Her own experience provides insight into the spiritual gifts of generational transitions.

> I feel much wiser than when I was younger and I feel more aware of things that could happen with my parents. I find I'm spending more time with my elders in Hinduism than I ever did before. When I was young, religion wasn't important for me. In my twenties, I did things as ritual but now I have a different orientation—I'm curious to understand the philosophy of it, so I use every chance I get to talk with elders.
>
> Earlier in my life I thought that our religion was rigid with women having a secondary status. But now that I'm older and considering how I've practised my religion, I admire how flexible it is. In fact, I see that there are many cases in which Hinduism has given women strength.
>
> My parents used to make sure that we did our evening prayers and I was a bit angry about that, wondering why we needed to do that. Why couldn't we be free? But when I think back now, I appreciate that more. The practice of our faith was always there.
>
> And now that I'm becoming an elder, I find that I'm looking forward to the grandparent stage of life. I now see my parents as having a lot of knowledge and experience and therefore a lot of power—like a superpower, as if God is in them. I'm so close to them lately and strongly believe that they bring a blessing to my life. They live in India and I'm in Canada but we talk every other day because I feel so close to them now. They give me a lot of comfort and I know they have faith in me. The distance and knowing I'm going to lose them may be heightening my sense of wanting to be

connected with them.

My parents always said, "Don't hold back anything against anyone and know that God is always there, watching." God is there, always watching you and that's why I must forgive. That's how we were always taught and I've internalized and practised that.

Nina's reflections underscore a number of points made by others: mid-life is a time for reawakening to the importance of what is spiritual; there's a mid-life urgency to spend time with and learn as much as we can from elders now that we realize that this time is limited; mid-lifers have the confidence to discern and appreciate what was valuable—or not—in what we learned from parents, while not necessarily adopting what they taught for ourselves; watching our parents as mid-lifers can inspire us to anticipate our own aging and grandparenting stage.

And, once again, a new understanding of how we have internalized and practised spiritual truths that we have been taught, leads us to think about how we are doing in relation to our own children, on our other side.

Although relationships with the older generation may be more comfortable than before, our relationships with our own children may be heading in another direction.

Fredelle told me:

I find that my relationship is somewhat more painful with my kids....I see my kids struggling with what to tell me and what not to bother telling me when we're together. And it's hard for me not to get back to whatever the chorus was with them—"Pick up your socks, or I wish you'd cut your hair, try harder, date more, date less, or whatever!" It may be that the kind of relationship I have with my parents won't be possible with my kids until they are in the middle.

Given that our children need to separate from us to complete the first part of their life journeys, the more we hang on, the more we seem to risk having a full and mature relationship with them into the future. Now that I have completed the first part of my journey, I can anticipate them doing the same. A longer view can help us live gracefully into these future possibilities.

*What are the older and younger people in your life teaching you about your mid-life soul?*

This helps me to accept that my own young adult children exhibit greater maturity and health the more distant they are from me. I do not take that to mean that I am a particularly difficult or demanding parent. I take it to mean that we become healthy and strong in the process of becoming adults apart from our family of origin, and that this movement needs to be supported with mid-life parental understanding. If we do so, our children will live their first journey of life well, in preparation for living their own middle and later journeys. There is joy as well as crisis in the process of finding a new role as parent.

Nina has found that her changing approach to parenting has allowed a new role for herself to emerge.

> I was very close to my children and mentally I have had to let go and distance myself. I needed to excuse myself and get ready for them to be gone. I am replacing physical care for them with prayer for their well-being because I've got to let them handle their life but I don't want them to suffer. I keep praying and find that through this I'm getting more and more into my role as religious elder. It's funny how you don't realize that you're doing it but, as you age, you naturally fall into the roles that your tradition taught you. And I strongly believe that, since I don't have my elders here in this country, we have to be the elders. It's essential for our children to have elders.

I am reminded of Margaret saying that her parents were teaching her how to age gracefully and we, as we become wise elders, are teaching our children how to do the same, by our actions and how we live into eldership.

Mary has come to the realization that the respect she wants from her mother is the same thing her daughters want from her, and it is not easy to give. She says:

It takes a lot of patience and the ability to step back and say "This is not totally my responsibility" when it comes to my daughters' problems. I have to realize that they are also adults and remember that I wanted my Mom to treat me as an adult. I'm still working on trying not to feel responsible for my daughters' decisions—or for my mother's decisions. I know this will bring freedom.

Mary may well have described the key to living well on the inside of the generational sandwich: respect both your parents and your children and do not take responsibility for their decisions and their lives. One's mid-life responsibility is to make good decisions for the middle, building upon the gifts and insights of the past. Such decisions will prepare us to make our decisions as elders.

Hugh describes how life's difficulties bring us into a new relationship with our adult children. A few years ago, he and his wife Carol, and their three young adult children were thrown together into a very frightening place as a result of Carol's cancer.

Our family life was deepened a few years ago when Carol went through breast cancer. Sideswipes of life are there to teach us that we don't have as much control over life was we think we have. This realization can either make us bitter or resentful or it can throw us into the arms of God where we're made more compassionate and loving and spiritually in tune to both the joy and pain of the world.

I remember us sitting together on the living room floor. Our kids were all there and we didn't know much yet about how far the cancer had spread. We sat there together; we held hands and laughed and prayed and cried. I thought we had been close before that but it doesn't get any better than this. It was like that old saying that you don't know what you've got until it's threatened.

Hugh's story inspires and challenges me to be open with my own adult children about threats to ourselves and our mortality as they arise. I am sure that I will have to fight a temptation to "protect" my children from such pain and yet mid-life vulnerability, as Hugh describes it, has the potential to help us all discover what we treasure in one another, across the generations.

Beth talks about how she's consciously acting more openly with her own children than her own parents did with her, for the sake of her children and her future relationships with them.

> When my grandmother got sick she disappeared up
> north and I was told that I shouldn't see her, and when she
> died I was told that I shouldn't go to the funeral because I
> should remember her as she had been. I felt left out.
>
> My own kids aren't sheltered like that, so part of what
> works in the middle is honesty. I don't hide what's going on
> with my parents or with my work or with my husband or
> my husband's work.

Beth sees this as one way in which she can respect the needs and experience of both the older and younger generations.

Mary expects that being a grandmother will involve fewer pressures than those involved in parenting and will, indeed, bring a new dimension to the sacred experience of family. Mid-life grandparents tend to confirm this expectation.

One of the things I hear them describe is that, as the physical demands of parenting subside, energy and spirit emerge to pursue interests that have been put on hold or not yet discovered during those years. Put simply, we have more time and energy available for other worthwhile endeavours.

Everyone in this chapter has shared wisdom about how to break through or prevent the cold wars that can erupt on either side of the mid-life experience, with parents or with children. Walls fall when we begin to understand and appreciate the rock from which we were hewn and the quarry from which we were dug and when we gain perspective on the kind of relationships we can initiate as mature adults. We can choose to nourish our own mid-life souls by learning from older ones who are aging and from letting go of trying to control those who are young, as we ourselves become elders. We can choose to see this process itself as a blessing.

# 5
# Getting It Together

**"To die a natural death, shouldn't that be every man's holy grail? No matter how long it lasted, nothing was shorter than a life."**

*Laurence Gough,* Memory Lane

*I*t began when I went back to summer camp as a thirty-eight-year old. A camp where I had been a counsellor, senior staff member, and director in my younger years asked if I would consider directing again. It seemed like a fine idea and my heart and soul bounced with anticipation. My body, on the other hand, was soon protesting.

I returned to the twenty-four hour demands of caring for a young community in the bush without giving any thought to the fact that I was now almost two decades older than when I had last done anything like this. In my mind's eye, it would be wonderful to be leading morning watch at the crack of dawn, participating in evening campfires, and counselling staff and campers 'round the clock. I did not anticipate any change from how it used to be—except that I was now much wiser!

Reality soon visited. I simply could not keep the same pace. I longed for seven or eight hours of nightly sleep to help me keep going. I had not needed to take care of my body like this when I was younger. I had been able to take it for granted, but that was no longer possible in the midst of such strenuous testing.

It is not as if I had been the picture of health when I was younger. Since childhood I have struggled with asthma and have a long track record of brokering deals with God: "If you just ease my breathing and get me through this demanding week, I promise, I'll slow down and take care of myself." God usually kept the divine side of the deal, sometimes with the assistance of drugs, but I rarely kept mine. I pushed my body from one assignment into the next, as long I was able.

But I am no longer able, as I began to realize during those summers at camp. The demands of the camp schedule required increasing drug use. Since the drugs enabled me to do more, I continued to maintain and often add to my heavy list of year-round responsibilities. I was running hard. But by the age of forty-two I knew that I had to make some changes. The medications weren't keeping pace with my growing physical distress (evidenced by worsening asthma). I had to consider making peace with my body and with God. Good intentions to take care of this very local, personal part of God's creation were no longer enough. I had to take action on those things over which I had the greatest control. By grace, I finally realized that I was travelling a road that—if left unchanged—would become most unpleasant. In a way, my body gave me no choice but to change. It was threatening divorce so I had to finally listen in a way that was unnecessary when I was younger.

This too is related to the typical mid-life awakening to mortality. Since I would not be able to live forever and accomplish everything I had imagined anyway, I had better slow down enough to live as well and as fully as God desired for me.

I no longer wanted to be dependent on medication even though this was one option. I decided that it could not hurt to listen to some alternative practitioners so that is what I did. I have been amazed at the results of changing my diet, doing Tai Chi, and meditating and walking regularly. I no longer rely upon drugs as I used to. They are still there to lean on for a while when I slip off the healthy road but I feel so much better without them. (Ironically, during the writing of this book I slipped far off the healthy road, ended up crashing, and needing drugs once again to get me back on track. The mid-life body simply demands to be taken seriously and, reawakened, I am taking it more seriously than ever before.)

*How has your body told you that you're in mid-life?*

Apart from this recent setback, I have never felt better. My body is no longer a problem child to be cajoled and pushed to get me through. My body is now a friend, teaching me about the benefits of balance, exercise, and simple, nutritious eating and drinking. My body has become essential to centring my soul.

Friendship with my bod·
perimenopause, the hormo
dramatic emotional ups a'
life depression. Yet even *
attention to the importa
taken for granted any l
have evidence that in\
and vitality.

I am reminded c
preoccupations wit
health becomes mor·
many mid-lifers, I kno\

Most told me that the·
changes. That is in fact how u..,
observations about mid-life being a time ·,
between life or death, seemed quite literally relevant ι.
passages as well.

Many, like Gerald, who had just turned fifty when I talked with him,
said things like

> I need to learn how to slow down. I'd better look after
> my body, not because I want to live longer, but because I
> want to live fully. I find that my legs are stiffer than they
> used to be after sitting in the car for only a short time, and
> when I get up in the morning the muscles are aching and it
> never used to be like this. I now realize it's part of the aging
> process.

By giving us no other option but to slow down or change our patterns
of consumption and activity, our bodies are giving us the opportunity to
learn some new things about our souls. First, reducing physical speed and
frenetic activity enables us to become more active in reflection. I like
walking better than running, not only because it is more comfortable but
because I now like moving at a pace at which I can notice the details. I
think better, with a greater sense of rhythm with the world, when I am
walking than when I am moving faster. This has become important to
my spiritual health as well as to my physical health. And accepting that I

efficient choices, according to what
y digest, has helped me become more
kin.

tunity to learn how body and soul are in
e abuse of one hurts the other; the care of one
When we choose to reject what is life-giving
ally, we make a choice for death that affects both.
to both physical and spiritual well-being we open a
w life.

*s your mid-*
*ody teaching*
*ur mid-life soul?*

I have never been completely surprised by studies that reveal how religious folks tend to live longer, healthier lives than others. This seems to me to be just more evidence of how attention to spiritual health affects physical health. Mid-life pushes us to think about our health in unprecedented ways. When mid-life friends are dying, we contemplate our own living.

Running 'til we hit the wall may have been our young adult goal but a mid-lifer who is still living this way risks serious damage at impact. As we become better acquainted with our bodies, learning how to scan for and reduce tension, we learn how to live and move with greater grace and efficiency. We will not waste precious energy.

I am not talking here about decline. I am talking about change or transformation. Just as I watch the development of my sons' young adult bodies with amazement, as they become increasingly muscular and strong, I have decided to view the changes in my own body with amazement too. This positive view has helped me to realize that my life does not need to diminish with physical change. It can be fulfilled. Yes, there are some new limits, but I have more opportunities to gain physical and spiritual health than ever before.

If I were to feel negatively about these changes or deny them, and put my energy into trying to reject or reverse change, I suspect that I would be less healthy as a result. I might end up spending my days trying to look young again or trying to escape reality through drug or alcohol abuse. My soul would die at least as quickly as my body.

Sybilla Mannsfeldt, who counsels mid-lifers, confirms that in mid-life our bodies slow down in order that we can become more active in reflection. This enables us to see the gifts we have been given by the creator and where they are needed in the creation. She says that we should be able to gently realize that we can not keep up with a pace set by a youth-obsessed society. In fact, she feels that North American society is particularly resistant to good and natural practices which she suspects are better accepted in other cultures. As a Baha'i, she feels that elders should be treated with more respect. Without cultural respect for the gifts that come with age, mid-lifers are forced to compete with younger folks on younger terms.

She thinks that her native Europe is somewhat better in its attitude to aging.

> I lived the first part of my life in Germany and I get the feeling that life is more enjoyed in Europe. Money isn't the only reason to be busy and in mid-life people can enjoy their lives. They get credit for wisdom and don't deny that they're celebrating their sixtieth and seventieth birthdays. There's more graciousness, even in clothing. In Germany there's a women's clothing size that translates as 'full slim' meaning more fully slim than a younger kind of slim. I see women there in their fifties who are dressed with nice designs for fuller figures but I don't see those choices here.

Let's face it, we do not look young anymore. If our souls embrace the culture's preference for youth, we find ourselves unsettled by what we see in the mirror. None of us wants to live up to the joke about middle age being when our broad mind and narrow waist change places. And while taking care of our bodies can keep body fat in check, our bodies *are* changing. When we see lines and wrinkles as proof of experience gained, we give ourselves an opportunity to embrace the wisdom of our souls.

Sybilla is working to help people recognize the cultural biases that we absorb into our own personal attitudes, in order to see that life with an older body can be great. "I want to be a catalyst for people so that they don't just dread old age and see everything in their life getting worse. I say 'don't die when the music's still in you!'"

She strongly suggests that consciously approaching aging with a positive attitude will determine mid-life health. Sybilla sees her work as helping people *grow* old as opposed to *getting* old. It takes courage, she says, to do conscious aging and you can change things in mid-life in order to have a better older life. The motivation to examine this need often comes in the wake of dramatic events like job loss and illness. And sometimes the lessons are very abrupt.

Judy S. is a palliative care nurse who brings insight into the body-soul connection both as a professional working with dying folks and as a mid-life person who has lived with cancer herself. I met Judy as a participant in a mid-life retreat which I led with Tim Scorer. Everyone who came to the retreat brought wisdom from which I learned, but what Judy had to say about coming to terms with her body particularly touched me. Her authority on the subject stemmed from having lived through a life-threatening disease. Being with her was an experience of being with someone who has come to a peaceful place through the changes.

Her mid-life reflections upon what her body has taught her soul began with changes that occurred before her cancer.

> I can remember quite distinctly when I turned fifty that I was comfortable in my own skin for the first time in my life. Before that, I'd always been critical of my shortness and my shape, but all of a sudden this settled down and I felt really empowered about who I was. My previous behaviour of going to the gym to try to change my body shape was no longer necessary. I could still go to the gym but with a different kind of energy. I had more pleasure, less apology, and less justification about who I was physically.
>
> Then breast cancer came as a blow at fifty-two. It was a shock. Cancer diagnosis was a total experience and I'm a changed person because of it. Not very much is the same in my life now as it was before. I found the lump small and it was treated soon and it was a type that wasn't as bad as some others. But because I'm a palliative care nurse, I know too much about this disease. I've attended too many funerals and lost too many friends who did all the right things. I knew that this was meant to be a wake-up call, an opportunity to change my life, a turning point. I didn't recognize all of this immediately. At first there was paralysis and

vulnerability and fragility. I went through a dark night of the soul and started reading and talking about it and some would say I was consumed.

Earlier in life you assume your body is who you are and that you know it pretty well, but then you find this lump—just the size of a pea—which they tell you has been growing for eight years. That's when I saw my body as a separate thing that I had to look after. I started talking with my body, asking what I could do to make it feel better. Before I was a mostly cerebral person—living from the neck up—but now I'm in a different relationship with my body. My body doesn't make the decisions, so I've got to take care of it, decide what to put into it and when it needs to float in a bubble bath. I'm much more aware of my body now. I scan for tension, breathe, and let it go. I believe in something called cellular memory—that once you've taught your cells a good practice, your body will let you know when you're not following it.

The drive towards integrity that we discussed in earlier chapters also leads us to address physical changes, threats, and opportunities. If I want to be a whole person, my body can no longer be ignored or treated as something unimportant to who I am. If I am going to live fully it will be in this body and this body needs attention.

Whether or not we have had to yet deal with mid-life physical problems, we know that we are tempting fate if we eat, drink, and worry as we did when we were younger. We are at greater risk of disease so we have to take prevention seriously. To gain integrity we must integrate all parts of ourselves with one another, including the physical.

We have already talked about the mid-life recognition that we are not in control of our lives as we once thought we were but, on the other hand, we also have the freedom to choose behaviours and practices that normally result in fullness of life and well-being.

Judy S. brings a refreshing perspective to letting go of any earlier needs to live according to "normal" standards. Cancer survivors likely understand this better than any others. I asked her about how her concept of "normal" had changed. "I learned that normal is just a setting on the dryer," she says, "and you're not supposed to go back to normal after this kind of experience. You're supposed to grow. I was given an opportunity to learn how to breathe, for one thing.

> I became a different kind of nurse, a much better caregiver. I became a wounded healer and that was quite a process. As I watched people die, I couldn't help but think about when this was going to happen to me.
>
> I know for sure that stress is like fertilizer for cancer and I had a responsibility to look at my stress level. I had been a single parent of two kids for twenty years, working full time. I looked at all that, realized that I could now make some choices with the kids at a different stage, and I wasn't going to stress myself anymore. For example, I became very focused in one-to-one encounters with people whereas before I was pushing myself through the day, looking at my watch, and not always taking time for lunch or even to go to the bathroom when I needed to. Nurses tend to ignore their bodies when there are so many demands, and I don't do that anymore.

Learning how to deal with stress is a crucial task of the mid-life soul—not that it is the first time in life when this is important. But now it seems no longer optional because our bodies are louder and more urgent in their demands—and the consequences of ignoring those demands are more severe. Back problems, arthritis or rheumatism, stomach trouble, high blood pressure or hypertension, as well as anxiety, depression, and other emotional difficulties are waiting close by—if not already regular visitors.

I am grateful that my body became demanding enough that I had to listen. As a result I have taken up physical and meditational practices that are beginning to calm and open me to the movement of the spirit in ways that were simply impossible when I was filled with stress that fed disease in both my physical and spiritual health.

The values of contemplation and meditation that so many mid-lifers have described in these pages are fully available to us only when the body accompanies the mind, allowing for the kind of deep relaxation that opens one's whole being to be in harmony with the vibrations of God's loved and loving creation.

When I slow my breathing and my body begins to feel warm and heavy, I feel myself held in God's care. I do not have to hold the world together because I and the world are already held. My best prayer and meditation time follows deep relaxation and Tai Chi. These exercises literally open me to energy from beyond my own physical boundaries and I feel myself connecting with all that is larger and loving. Energy flows through me and I can both receive and contribute loving thoughts to the larger web of life. When I have not taken the time for physical preparation, prayer simply does not feel as complete or effective for myself, and I suspect, for those for whom I am praying.

As I listened to Judy S. I knew I was listening to someone who understands and lives this way of being. I also felt that I was listening to someone who has overcome fear of death.

> Meditation and deep relaxation give you the chance to let the stuff that causes stress to drift to the periphery. It will be there as you need it but you don't need it in that moment. I don't need to fear what will come into the space I create in meditation. I just assume that it will be good and it is always at least restful if not inspiring.

Judy has applied what she has learned not only to her own health but to the ways in which she is an agent of healing as a palliative care nurse. She has become a practitioner of therapeutic touch, which has opened up the channels of her own soul as well as others'.

> In doing therapeutic touch I receive as much as I give...even if I'm just there as a brow-stroker. I start by saying a prayer to ask God to use me to bring rest and relief, and I keep silently saying the person's name throughout—to keep other thoughts out of the way. You can't be involved in the outcome because that's the ego at work and that's not what this is about. You just offer the gift and something may or may not happen. I pray for that too—to be open and not to tell God what to do.

I believe, as Judy does, that a deep commitment to healing and

physical health is ultimately linked to a commitment to our spiritual
health. I also believe that her resulting practice of focusing upon the well-
being of others reveals a key to one's own healing and health. And her
experience reminds us that the physical story of mid-life does not need to
be about weakening and decline, but rather about change, acceptance,
the discovery of new strengths, vitality, and gifts for sharing.

Sheldon, a long-time television producer accustomed to the fast-
paced, stressful life of putting out a weekly television program, spoke to
me about how it has become much more critical for him to listen to his
forty-eight-year-old body now than at any earlier time in his life. We
spoke in a nice coffee house, at a slower pace than usual, away from the
frenzy of the television studio. In this relaxed setting he reflected upon
how his new-found mid-life approach to listening to his body is related to
the way he plans and lives all of his life differently than he used to.

> You have to be careful about how you develop strategies
> for your life because the extent to which you do this may be
> the extent to which you lose consciousness with the here
> and now. Strategies come with predisposed values and
> feelings and fears, based upon your life history and
> experience. If you were burned last time—or if you had a
> good time last time—you create a strategy based on that
> past. That makes strategy immediately obsolete because it's
> based upon the past and not the present. One of the ways of
> dealing with this tendency is to listen to your body. If you
> listen to your body and try to get your body and mind in
> sync with one another, in balance and travelling together,
> you are better able to be conscious of the present and you
> don't have the same stresses that result in all kinds of
> diseases, from colds to God-knows-what.

I understand Sheldon to be saying that greater body awareness is one
of the ways in which the mid-life soul is helped to move on from the first
part of life's journey, to live in the present, more fully and more consciously. The body can help rescue the soul from becoming trapped in
strategies tied to the past. In other words, it can be an ally in fulfilling the
soul's desire to live in new and different ways.

Sheldon's experience also echoes a recognition that greater physical limits can mean a greater awareness of how to do things more sensibly and efficiently.

> I think when I was younger I felt a kind of invincibi-
> lity—a sense of energy that made me think I could do pretty
> well anything. I could do an all-nighter but I'd still be okay.
> I'd get a second wind the next day. And now, in my late
> forties, if I have one or two glasses of wine too many, I feel it
> the next day.
> I have a young child so I spend a lot of time on the floor.
> While I still get up with reasonable efficiency I know that
> I'm not bouncing up the way I used to. It's not that there's
> anything I can't do that I used to do, but it's different. I
> have to be more conscious of what I'm doing and how. I
> have to do things more gradually and handle life situations
> differently than I used to....I also have to cope with denial
> and a tendency to say "it's not really happening" because it is
> happening.

I think Sheldon makes an important point. There is absolutely no reason to suggest that mid-lifers can not take on any particular activity. In fact, as a result of a thoughtful approach to exercise, I am more physically active and feel better than I did a decade ago. However, this is a result of paying attention to what I can do and where I have met limits. I did not have to even think about limits twenty years ago—the body's stamina and agility were just there and unquestioned. I know that I have to work myself up to a week of strenuous hiking. I can not just go out and start trekking on a nice summer's day if I have not been walking regularly throughout the winter and spring. When I do not think about it ahead of time, and try to do it anyway, at some level denying my mid-life physical realities, my body is harsh in its reminders—I feel weak and stiff for a week.

Judy R. is a playwright, journalist, and teacher. We chatted after sharing an invigorating aqua-fit class. Her awakening to the intimate relationship between body and soul, the physical and the spiritual, came during the seven years in which she cared for her dying mother.

The person I was when I started caring for my mother
and the person I was when I finished were completely
different. At the beginning all I saw were my mother's
practical needs and I made sure she got her food and
whatever else she needed. But her emotional needs were left,
and I began to realize that her emotional needs were more
important than getting the meal on time. During those
seven years I began going to mid-life retreats and got
spiritual direction and my writing started to take off and all
kinds of positive things were happening, but boy, was I
struggling! There were times when I wanted to somehow
escape the difficulty of it all but my spiritual director would
just keep saying to me, "Stay in it, stay in it" and that was
the best advice she could have given me. It felt like hell. I felt
I was in a prison camp at times—even though my mother is
a positive person—but still, the situation was overwhelming.

Trying to avoid the unprecedented physical or emotional challenges
that confront us at mid-life is not the way to something better. This too
reveals an important marker in the mid-life discovery of the soul. Looking for the opportunities to learn through them, by staying engaged and
getting the help we need to get perspective, is the hopeful course. Judy
did precisely this. She pursued the kind of spiritual direction that would
help her learn from the great challenge of caring for her dying mother.
She also decided that she needed to engage her body in this process.

A teacher of the martial arts gave her a fresh new perspective on the
relationship between body and soul—one that would forever change her
life in the middle.

I decided to study karate. I had all this anger built up
and I sure didn't want to take it out on my mother, so
instead I beat up fourteen-year-olds! One of the things my
sensai taught me was that we are not bodies encasing souls
but rather that the soul encases the body. We are the soul!
He also used to talk about how the body is the house—my
house—but the soul, the energy, the spirit that gives it life, is
encompassing the body. I see body and soul as one now and

the integration point for me is stillness. When you approach
movement from the point of view of stillness, as you do in
the martial arts, there's an integration that you don't find if
you just haphazardly do things. And it really helps to get rid
of anger.

Over and over again, mid-lifers described how their bodies help them
make connections with their souls, after paying attention to their bodies,
and when they come to recognize value in stillness as well as action. I find
the imagery that Judy's sensai creates to be very helpful and engaging.

Taking my mid-life body seriously is just another way of facing my
physical limits in time as well as in ability. When I imagine my body
surrounded by my soul, I see my body as limited but my soul around it as
unlimited. My physical limitations in terms of what I can do physically
before I die, with capacities that are different from those of my youth, are
real. But at the same time I'm discovering that my soul is not limited in
these ways. It is linked with other souls of all times and places and
together we are linked with God's unlimited love.

Again, I am speaking about transformation rather than simple decline
and I think that this is how all of life works. We begin as babies with the
potential to develop sophisticated physical capacity, which we do
throughout our young years. Intellectual and emotional capabilities
follow physical development in their own time. The physical changes of
mid-life appear to provide a catalyst for a transformation towards greater
spiritual maturity. As in every life stage to this point, we are given
opportunities to develop new capabilities, but we have to decide whether
we want to embrace maturity or run from it.

Whatever doubts I may have had about the power of prayer when I
was younger are long gone. The world changes every day due to the
tireless, physical efforts of those who take on causes and work hard to
launch political, visible action. But I often wonder how much prayers for
peace, which are often offered by those who cannot be so physically
active, also have an effect. Millions around the world offered prayers to
end the Cold War. Who is to say that their attention to the limitless part
of themselves—their souls and how they aligned their souls—was not as
effective as demonstrations and other very visible work? These are the
musings of a mid-life soul that has listened carefully to others and has the

sense that there is truth in their insights.

Another gift in the sensai's image of our souls wrapping our bodies is the thought that our souls can care for our bodies. Mid-life souls have increasing wisdom for our bodies, as we have already described—slow down, use your limited physical abilities in the best ways possible, do not waste your efforts on what is unimportant and stressful, and discover new ways of enjoying your body and its capacity for regeneration and healing.

Just as no house of God *contains* God, no body *contains* the soul. But, like the house, the body gives us a place in which to focus on the connections with what is outside and around.

*What image would you use to describe how you see the relationship between your mid-life body and soul?*

It is the body through which we listen as well as speak, through which we drink in all of the textures of what is to be seen, smelled, touched, enjoyed, and engaged with in this world. Now that I am paying more attention to the connections between the physical and the spiritual, I am enjoying my body more than ever.

Even in the natural progress of their limitations, our bodies are teaching us of our need for interdependence. When I must find my glasses to read what my children have just handed me for comment, or when I have to ask for conversational nuggets to be repeated because I did not hear them the first time, I become more aware of my dependence on the patience and help of others. I believe that this dependence also enables me to be more patient with others than I ever was at a younger age.

Not only am I helped when others search with me for my glasses and bring patience in repeating what they have said, but I am relying more than I ever did on that kind of patience when I have once again lost my keys or misplaced my datebook—experiences that I can not remember having when I was younger.

But then my memory is not so great anymore either! During a mid-life retreat that I was leading a few years ago, many questions were raised about memory. These were first identified in gender group discussions. We identified our own particular mid-life concerns as women and as men and also listed questions that we had for those in the other group.

When women met alone, memory loss emerged as a deeply troubling mid-life experience. We wondered if the loss was the result of menopause

and decided to ask the men if this was something
that ever happened to them. When we came back
together to talk about our concerns and questions,
we asked them about this. To our surprise, memory
loss had been high on their list of concerns as well.
My interviews with mid-life men have confirmed
that they share this experience and concern.
Recently I heard a doctor use the term

*What life-giving
changes are your
body and soul
challenging you
to embrace?*

"andropause" to describe what happens to men in mid-life. He said that a
gradual drop-off in hormones accounts for loss of muscle strength,
cardiac problems, fatigue, irritability, and trouble with concentration.

Sheldon brought insight into how this too, can be a way in which our
mid-life bodies and minds teach our souls.

> I have a good memory for long-term things, for things
> that happened years ago, but sometimes now I forget names
> and that never used to happen, or I forget what I was doing
> and find myself returning to the room where I had my first
> thought about what I was going to do, as if I left it there.
> This is a more frequent experience now, with more of these
> things slipping. The first thing I feel when this happens is a
> sense of panic. I mean, this is the kind of thing that can have
> you in the street one day without knowing where you are!
> But then the second thing I feel is "Oh well, what is, is."
> And sometimes the very act of relaxing about it and being
> able to control the anxiety changes what you can recall.
>
> One of two things can come out of this experience of
> forgetting and feeling less in control. One is just to say
> "That's just the way it is and it's not going to change." But
> another thing that can happen is that you can learn how to
> wait. Waiting isn't retreating or surrender. Waiting is a lot
> like listening. And when you listen to your body and mind
> and you don't put anxiety into the question of "When am I
> going to remember?" sometimes the gate is removed and
> you do remember. It doesn't always work but it's a helpful
> frame of mind.
>
> We rush around into so many things and there's less time

in a day because we're running so hard to do so much. We aren't inclined to recognize the skill of waiting which has been so important to eastern thinking for centuries. We need more of it—it's in *our* scriptures too. Sometimes new openings can come through waiting, through contemplation.

Although Sheldon is Jewish, he has also been very influenced by studying eastern religions and by Christianity.

I have really vivid experiences of listening to something that's greater than I am but I don't know what to call it. I'm not hearing voices but I'm hearing something in my mind and more often than not I feel that it's God-given and God-driven, something that's far wiser and greater than I, for which I have no explanation.

For example, the last time I saw my mother was just over two years ago. I was standing by her hospital bedside, kissed her good-bye, and said I hoped to see her soon, not really coming to terms with the fact that this might be it. I had my young daughter with me and everything seemed to slow down. I looked over to her, picked her up, lowered her down so she and my mother could kiss one another. My mother was weak and connected to all kinds of tubes but as we walked away she gave a very exuberant wave. As I walked down the hall a voice inside said "This could be it—get back in there!" but I didn't listen to it. I didn't know then how to take that extra step and accept that voice.

While ultimately I think it was okay with my mother, it wasn't okay with me. And I feel this kind of thing more often than I did when I was younger. I think a lot of it has to do with slowing down—not always by choice—and just listening. And sometimes you get this little gift, this little insight and moment of clarity. That's when the challenge begins. When it happened with my mother I just didn't know what to do with it. I think one of the greatest sadnesses in the human condition is when we have an opportunity like that—which only comes once—and we don't take it. I take some comfort in that my mother took the opportunity. She knew.

I started studying eastern religions in my youth and while I learned about all this intellectually, I didn't live it until now, because now my body has led me to it. I believe that my studying and learning in my twenties and thirties was groundwork for me to accept what I'm learning now. For me to be working out five times a week and pushing myself hard is a virtual impossibility and would be about living in a place of denial. What's important is to accept the aging process and learn from it in order to transform or convert this experience into a feeling that these are great years! It's about converting fear and anxiety about aging into an awareness that this is a great time!

Knowing that the sun is behind those clouds is a pretty low level of faith but faith in the face of controversy and difficulty builds fibre and encourages people to do incredible things. I'm more in touch with the things I would call faith at this time in my life, and more in touch with what I would call God.

Once again, Sheldon's words point to the mid-life potential for coming to see that which knows no limits, through the experience of facing our own, physical limits. Throughout all of these mid-life conversations and stories, there is a realization that the youthful body is lost, yet a sense of eternal spirit can be gained in a body that has been forced to slow down, either by dramatic illness or by gradual change.

*What spiritual strengths are emerging for you in conjunction with these physical changes?*

Healing, salvation, and wholeness are accessible to the mid-life soul that recognizes new opportunities in the midst of new limitations.

Learning how to breathe, care for the body, wait, contemplate, act efficiently, and share truth about the changes and challenges with others are emergent directions for the mid-life journey. They are keys to mid-life liberation and vitality.

*6*

# Return on Investment

**"A woman living in a grand house may pride herself on all her lovely things, but the moment she hears the crackle of fire she decides very quickly which are the few she values most."**

*Arthur Golden*, Memoirs of a Geisha

One of the saddest things about working on this book was listening to mid-lifers who feel trapped in what they are doing, with a gnawing sense that they should now be living and working with greater generosity but are somehow held back by worldly obligations. I am not talking just about people whom I formally interviewed but also about many other informal conversation with mid-lifers over the past few years. Struggles often came to light when I asked questions about how mid-lifers can be blessings to others, after receiving a half-life of blessings themselves.

These have not been easy questions for me to work through either. Mid-life is a time when we are often still carrying many responsibilities. We may be worried, for example, about parents as well as children. Who knows what financial help parents may need or what the final educational bill for our children's successful launch will look like? And what about all of the reports saying we will need to have millions of dollars in savings in order to remain healthy and independent? It is frightening to think about severing reliable sources of good income even when the work does not seem to be accomplishing or contributing as much as it once did, or when it is not nourishing one's soul as it once did.

I suspect that I have only begun to work out the answers to these questions in my own life but already I feel some progress. Thinking about how my life's blessings translate into offerings, has helped me to see and be more open to go to the places where I am needed. I have been surprised at the ways in which God has provided throughout this process. Having climbed out of comfortable work routines, new opportunities for work that are a good match between the world's needs and my own have simply emerged, and I feel richly blessed in this new cycle of life.

Frederick Buechner's words about vocation have become extremely important to me. In *Wishful Thinking: A Seeker's ABC*, Buechner says, "The place God calls you is the place where your deep gladness and the world's deep hunger meet."

*What are some of the ways in which you can imagine your deep gladness and the world's deep hunger meeting?*

His advice resonates to a mid-life soul's realization that, while society's call may no longer satisfy, neither does the call of self-interest. We want our lives to count for something and we know we do not have forever to make that happen. We also long for a deep sense of joy and resonance with something larger than ourselves.

We desire our outer lives to reflect our inner lives, adding another dimension to our now-familiar theme of the mid-life drive to integrity. And for those who take their spiritual lives seriously, this means that we care as much about the integration of God's world as our own selves.

I am still in the midst of coming to terms with this mid-life calling to discern what I am here to do and to let go of whatever bondage is holding me back from doing it, trusting that God will provide. God *has* provided in the past, whenever I have leapt in the direction of meeting the world's hunger, but it is still a difficult leap. I also know that to ignore the call to look outward would stunt my soul's growth. I have seen too many mid- and later-lifers who have drawn their circles so small that they appear to care only for their close friends and family. It seems as if they have lost compassion for anyone or anything beyond and they do not look like deeply happy people.

In writing this book I expected to meet a lot of people who had turned their backs on the youthful markers of success (wealth, in large part) and I did meet some. But the seemingly common dilemma of feeling trapped by material obligations and a fear of the future without an adequate pension remains a frequent theme.

I believe that this represents more than a
personal spiritual crisis—it is a social crisis for us as
North Americans. A wise old prairie woman told
me a few years ago that if we believe no one will be
there to help us when we are old, we will likely
behave in a way that creates a society where no one
is. We will continue to focus upon our own

*How does the
difference between
bondage and
responsibility look
in your life?*

personal survival and acquisition of wealth and lose sight of how we are
impoverishing our communities, ourselves, and the legacy we are leaving
our children.

Financial advisors see us as a prime market for wanting to get a good
return on investment. Maybe so, but I believe that something deep inside
also calls us to want to deliver a good return on the investments that have
been made in us. We want to leave the world in better shape than we
found it.

While there may be mid-lifers who have lost hope in their ability to
follow their desires and to concentrate on being a blessing to the world, I
talked with a number of individuals who are living spirited, hope-filled
lives and have listened to what makes that possible for them.

One of the things I heard from people both inside and outside
Christianity is that it is impossible to list those behaviours that are clearly
good or clearly not. Many Christians have been profoundly shaped by
theologian Paul Tillich's description of sin as the state of separation—
from oneself, from others, and from God. I find Tillich's view particularly
enlightening with reference to mid-life. As we have seen from preceding
pages, we are no longer satisfied to be separated—"dis-integrated"—from
ourselves or from God, and while we may often feel the need for retreat,
we do not ultimately desire retreat to separate us from the rest of the
world. Although we have felt the world's push to become "self-sufficient"
or "independent," by now experience has taught us that we are intimately
connected to every part of creation. Amazing patterns of ecological
relationships, including those we share with other people, make it very
clear that how we choose to live affects the world, for better or worse.
Mid-life souls feel challenged to pay attention to their growing inner
voices that long for good connections with others and with the earth.

Although some might assume that a more meditative, reflective life results in wanting to avoid the world, my own experience and what I've heard from others suggest that it does the opposite. Contemplation leads us further into engagement with the world. I recently returned from a twenty-four hour silent retreat, amazed by the clarity and energy that I had received for my work. Ironically, at mid-life it may be necessary to look inward in order to see the outward world in a clearer way. In our younger years we focused on what we needed from the world; now our orientation can be to discern what the world needs from us.

Flora Litt describes what is happening through this process, from her own perspective as a Christian.

It's that spark of the divine within us—our higher self that wants to accomplish what we came here to do. We want to fulfill our soul's desire, our deepest desire. And God has said "I will give you your deepest heart's desire." Joseph Campbell said "Get in touch with your yearning—your deepest yearning and ask what is your bliss?" We need to ask this question in middle life because it's a way of fulfilling our higher being, our made-in-the-image-of-God self. And I believe that when we put our foot on this path we have all the energy of the universe behind us and doors open up. Opportunity opens to take a needed course, for example, or a friend who needs loving arrives on our doorstep. Opportunities come when we open up to life!

The greatest decision in mid-life has to do with deciding whether to turn in upon one's self or to turn outward toward others, regardless of where those others may be, whether they're in one's community or on the other side of the world.

It's a time when we should feel increasing freedom, not a sense of bondage. There's a difference between fulfilling responsibility and being in bondage.

Flora's distinction between bondage and responsibility is most helpful. At mid-life I no longer choose to take on obligations that are not life-giving in some way. I will, however, choose to fulfill responsibilities that are rooted in my gladness and another's need.

Munir brings a faith-filled perspective to the long and mysterious course of our spiritual lives. Munir was a pre-medical student at American University in Beirut when war broke out and he had to leave in a hurry. He came to Canada twenty-three years ago, when he was twenty years old. He had to deal with the same frustration that many professionals from other countries experience when rejected in a foreign land. Some lose hope, take menial jobs, turn to welfare, or return home. But he persevered and is now a dentist. His deep faith appears to be the main reason for his ability to find his way.

> From early in my life I was a so-called practising Muslim. I lived in a household where practising our Islam was part of my life and I think that affected me so that when I came to Canada, with a number of challenges, I was able to look at the ultimate objective of life which I basically learned from my faith.
>
> From an Islamic perspective once life starts, it does not come to an end. There are four phases of life, one after the other, so that whatever happens is placed in the proper perspective. The four phases are: birth; the second phase; death, which is a time of waiting for the fourth phase of life; and, finally, life in eternity.

Munir's clear sense that his mid-life is located early within a life process that is linked with his eternal life immediately provides him with a larger perspective. I find it instructive that both Flora and Munir are able to locate their sense of joy and purpose within a more comprehensive view of their place in a spirit-filled universe. Their personal purpose and joy is intimately woven into a larger tapestry.

Munir also sees the threat of bondage that comes with privilege, and the subsequent challenge in it. "As a Muslim I am a firm believer that life goes on and that God almighty will distribute our share of trials and tribulations as he sees fit. Sometimes people think they're being privileged when in fact they are being tested with these privileges.

> As a child in Lebanon, I was always longing for a more comfortable life. I remember seeing images on television

about life in America. But today I feel stronger in my faith
and I am enjoying the spirituality which my faith is offering
me. It's not an image but it's a reality that I've experienced
and I want to show others how to live their spirituality to
the fullest and enjoy life. This doesn't mean that I don't get
ill or lose money or have difficulties or unpleasant arguments. I live my life like anyone else. But it seems I am now
more capable of coping with these things. Life is a system
whereby you build on your past, and now in my middle age
I can see this cumulative process more clearly and am able to
share it with others.

Munir suggests that a mid-life move away from valuing superficial
privilege to building a stronger spiritual life enables one to better cope
with mid-life difficulties. He goes on to describe how a mid-life spiritual
perspective helps him take a longer view of giving and receiving.

In the past I was on the receiving end but now it's
different. I saw a very needy patient in my dental clinic. I
knew she couldn't afford the treatment which she needed
and I was happy just to provide her with it. If I had charged
her it would have earned me $600. The very next day I
finished a big project for another patient and when I
presented her with the cost to which she had agreed, she
looked at me and said, "Doctor, I can see that you've worked
very hard on this and you've made me so happy that I want
to give you $500 more." She insisted.

I use this as an example of giving that comes back
unexpectedly. These things happen but we don't always see
the connection between what happened yesterday and
today. But for me, within the framework of spirituality, I feel
that God is part of my everyday life and all of the little
things that happen to me. I want to live as a Muslim to the
fullest so when I see something beautiful, my response is to
praise God. I surround myself in my dental office with
things such as the words from the Koran that remind me
that my spirituality is part of my life.

I suspect that people who have so fully
embraced the teachings of their faith, surrounding
and reminding themselves of these teachings,
have an advantage when it comes to hearing and
accepting God's call in the confusing middle of life.
They know that they are located in something
larger and loving. There are reference points by which to gain one's
bearings. "Calling" is the word that people often used in these
conversations, even though God's calling is a difficult experience to
describe and define.

*What mid-life risks do you feel "called" to take?*

Hugh has thought a lot about this. He's executive director of a social
service agency and has worked with individuals, families, and organiza-
tions in all kinds of settings over the years. His religious experience began
in the Catholic church, was nurtured through Inter-Varsity Christian
Fellowship while in university and, since then, in Anglican, United, and
Baptist churches. It has never been about the denomination, he says, but
rather about the help he has found in these churches, and he is especially
pleased now to be part of a house church within his local parish.

> I thought I was in mid-life when I went back to school at
> thirty-eight. I could have stayed where I was at that point,
> had security and a good retirement and all that. But I was
> reading about taking risks so I took a risk. A sense of calling
> had always been important for me, so I did it! We sold our
> house, went to Quebec City so I could study and then I
> started all over again at forty. I had nothing materially but
> was much richer than when I had started. And not only was
> I richer, but my kids and wife were too, for a number of rea-
> sons that were spiritual and also based in what we learned.
>     I was able to spend two years studying about what's
> hurting people in organizations and the small piece that I
> can bring to healing in that situation. When I finished I
> went to work in the provincial ministry of health and saw
> people who were wounded, yet held by security. Their souls
> were dead but they kept on because they were too scared to
> move out. I continue to work to bring heart and soul and
> spirit to all kinds of organizations.

Hugh continues to be intrigued by this question of what holds some people in familiar and often dysfunctional work settings while others come to the point of feeling the threat of spiritual disintegration and choose to break free, especially at mid-life. His work in this area is made more impressive by his own ability to continually re-examine and take action on his own need to take risks.

I'm now forty-nine and I think there's another mid-life time coming, because I'm starting to feel restless again. It's not as unsettling as the first time but it may be to a deeper calling. That calling comes from a struggle with my faith and what it means in my life. I can tell you intellectually and theologically what I believe but to move that to my heart and into my gut is where the real struggle is. You never know how many years you have left to live and the restlessness and struggle now are about what kind of legacy I want to leave, and how I can come to a deeper calling in my life so that I can help others go through that. I agree with whoever said "You can only bring people as far as you are yourself."

*What spiritual practices do you intend to use so that you may be sustained in your risk taking?*

Hugh's vocational struggles take place within a prayerful life that itself has evolved and is different at mid-life than it was when he was young. "My prayers now are more cries of frustration, pain, and joy and, like talking to a friend, from the centre of my being. Most of us 'live lives of quiet desperation' and I've learned how to cry it out to God. God's not going to fall apart and neither am I. I'm not afraid to express doubt now."

Hugh's experience of risking and living fully, often on the edge, has placed him in a position to learn how to move from dwelling on his own pain to responding to others, with compassion. Decades of life experience can be brought into focus within the discomfort of an open mid-life soul.

It's a stripping away of all these silly ideas of what life is all about. It's not about material things or status or about how many degrees you have after your name. It's not about any of that but it's about dying to yourself and letting God live through you so you can leave a legacy for this world. That's easy to say but that's what it's all about. We have our God, we have our life, we have our legacy. I think mid-life is a beautiful way to use experience to allow music to come from us, music built upon our gifts, who we are as human beings and what we have to give to others.

The older I get the more reflective I've become and the more mellow. I've been a very angry person for a lot of my life because of my family background and the fact that my father left when I was a baby. I guess I felt like the world owed me more. I don't think that way now. Now I'm starting to think about what I can give to the world with the gifts that have been given to me. No one in my family went to university and I got to get a good university education. Yes, I decided to do it, but people opened doors for me. And I'm very grateful that I've had a long marriage and an intact family, that I've been able to know God in some small measure. On my best days I'm just very grateful!

Gratitude is not the only available mid-life response to years of painful life experience. And, of course, every mid-life soul has known years of painful experience. It seems, however, that gratitude may be one of the most healing, most constructive responses we can have, for our own sakes and for others'. It's what keeps us going and catapults us into giving again and again.

I met Lynn at a mid-life retreat a few years ago, and was deeply moved by her story. Her mid-life transition was in a most deep and most difficult place, yet her gratitude and joy remain unconquered. She had known an almost unbearable pain. Lynn's son had taken his own life and every part of *her* life was now turned inside out. Recently, she spoke with me about how she has been able to find new wells of joy, new direction in her life, and a sense of what she has to give.

There's a prayer that I read every night for a year. It begins: "When sorrow comes, let us accept it simply, as a part of life. Let the heart be open to pain; let it be stretched by it." It restored my sense of stillness and a deepening of meaning that leads to dedication. You can't move forward without that peace.

Lynn has certainly allowed herself to be stretched by her pain. She and her husband and other son have travelled through their tragedy together and have come out of it with a sense of wonder. She refers to her first child as their "shadow child" who has not completely left them and still accompanies them. Once again, her perspective on tragedy has turned to how to share her blessings.

> I have been a very lucky person. We're much different than we were but we've come through it. We've been blessed and I don't know how I'd have made it through without the wonderful people I've been given. If ever I was going to say "I've seen the face of Christ," it was when I was in the psych ward and a schizophrenic stayed up all night to listen to me. Some people go through their whole lives without being given such a gift of compassion. But when you receive it you understand what a gift it is and that it cannot be kept. It would lose its value if you tried to keep or hold it. It has to be given back.

*What blessings are you most grateful for and how might these be transformed into blessings for others?*

Lynn's deep sense of needing to give back the gift of compassion is related to her decision to work towards a new career. Until recently she worked for many years in the real estate unit of an oil company. She approved contracts and supervised twelve people.

> I was always uncomfortable and felt untrue to myself. I knew this work wasn't a good fit. But you go ahead because bills have to be paid. I was competent but I couldn't get excited about finding an error in a clause.
>
> After we lost Russell there wasn't any reason to continue. The job had paid for his tutoring before but now I found it

harder and harder to play the game if all it promised was the possibility of moving into a better house or something. Who cares about that?

I think everybody knows when something's wrong and you're not in rhythm with yourself. When the rhythm is right, life is like a dance but when it's wrong, you're stepping on others' toes—and even on your own. We all need to take a breath and give ourselves the chance to see what we should be doing and give ourselves the permission to just do it. Even though I was doing the wrong dance I couldn't stop. I allowed somebody else to be the maestro and you should never let anyone else be your conductor. You may not have to live to mid-life to listen to yourself but I had to have the confidence that came in mid-life to do it.

Lynn's desire to make her career change became clearer during a mid-life retreat, but she didn't want to just say "I quit" without working this through with her husband. "We had both come from the wrong side of the tracks and he had a fear about having enough money."

So Lynn decided to give her husband the gift of a mid-life retreat for himself. He became clearer about what he was going through and as a result he could see what she was going through. They were then able to work out a new image of the future, together. She's gone back to school to become a social worker. When she is finished, it will be his turn to pursue a new career path.

I like Lynn's dancing imagery very much. We are finally ready in mid-life to examine and choose for ourselves the music to which we will dance. And every kind of dance includes moving in and moving out. Moving inward, through retreat and reflection, prepares us to move outward. And while our mid-life steps outward might not look as dramatic as our youthful steps once did, perhaps we have gained some grace. Lynn finds it interesting to see the differences between herself and her young classmates.

I think I have more tolerance and more life experience. I don't see things in black and white terms as much as the younger students do. They are so passionate and see things

so clearly. And I'm passionate but don't see things so clearly
at all. I say "Yes, but you can see what's on the other hand"
and they say, "No, we can't!'

Mentoring younger students has brought her great joy and is one of
the ways in which she has discovered how her own experience can be
returned, as a gift. And her own experience of losing her son has enabled
her to provide unique support to others, including to a woman whose
daughter recently died. But Lynn's view of how to change the world as a
mid-lifer is quite different from when she was a young adult, and her
experience is echoed by others. People spoke to me with mid-life
conviction about the importance of contributing in small ways more than
in large schemes. As Lynn put it,

> When I was eighteen, I was going to save the world. I'm
> not naïve enough to think I'm going to save the world now
> but I know I can at least help somebody help themself.

Others said similar things. You met Judy R. in an earlier chapter. As a
playwright and journalist she has dedicated years to the challenge of social
reform, and her perspective has matured in mid-life.

> I'm not as idealistic as I used to be. I'm more realistic
> about what I can change and what I can't. I don't try to break
> down walls that I know aren't going to fall down. I'm more
> strategic, wanting to get inside to find out where the power is
> and try to influence that power.
>       And I think mid-life is about realizing that you have to do
> the work. You can't expect somebody else to do it anymore—
> you've got to do it. The buck stops here. That's a mid-life
> realization for me. I've always been kind of responsible but
> didn't used to feel like I was in charge. Now I feel that I am
> in charge and I have to do some work here. Part of that
> attitude comes from being an orphan and thinking "I'm the
> last generation now—I'd better get moving!"

Something happens to you when you read the newspapers and realize that the people making national and international policies are no longer older than you are. When there no longer is an older, wiser generation to lean on for making the tough decisions and doing the hard work, it becomes our own, as Judy suggests. Some mid-lifers will decide that now is the time to get involved with systemic changes and others will make commitments to individuals and causes closer at hand. Once again, discerning how our gladness and the world's needs meet, comes back to knowing ourselves better.

Flora Litt says more about this.

> We give according to our personality and style so we do need to turn in to look and listen and ponder what that is, but not to stay turned in upon ourselves in a narcissistic way. Whatever we were like earlier in our lives is more accentuated in mid-life and I believe that's because it's raised up to be healed. This is an opportunity for transformation and it's not a time to be fearful.

Every person of faith with whom I spoke, from any of a variety of traditions, seemed to be profoundly shaped by beliefs that God cares both for our personal health and also for the health and healing of the world. It was strongly suggested that personal wholeness is indeed one of the by-products of care for, and work towards, the healing of the community, whether it be local or global.

Flora added a comment about what we particularly have to contribute to this healing, as mid-lifers. "I feel strongly that by the time we get to mid-life we've learned a few things about ourselves, about life and love, and we have things to share out of that."

Now is the time to assess our lives in relation to our view of more ultimate purposes, in relation to what brings us deep gladness and what the world hungers for, our own style of giving, the blessings inherent in the pain of our own life experiences and how we can transform those blessings into our legacy.

# Conclusion: Abundant Life— Playing on the Slide

**"…for you are with me…"**

*Psalm 23, verse 4*

Within our mid-life retreats Tim and I invite participants to announce their birth into life's second journey. This is scheduled near the end of a reflective week and they typically do this with joy and celebration. Unlike their first birth announcements, relatively few include birth weight! However, they write these announcements on their own terms now, as they decide what is important for the world to know. It is a way of marking the end of life's first journey and the beginning of a new adventure.

In all of the attention placed on mid-life crisis and angst, I do not believe joy has received its rightful share of ink. Increasing freedom, new-found confidence, and a new kind of energy have been expressed in these pages as much as confusion and depression.

Paul was exuberant when he told me:

> At forty-two years old, to finally be able to say "I am happy" is quite an experience. It's not that there haven't been moments of happiness before, but now there's a deep sense of completeness and happiness and joy and celebration— this is who I am!

My first working title for this book was *It's All Downhill from Here* and while I prefer *Soul Maps*, I like the paradoxical nature of the first title. We use this expression in two different ways. Sometimes we use it as a positive expression: it's all downhill means we can coast, there's no effort required. On the other hand, sometimes we use it negatively: it's all downhill means things are deteriorating. Mid-life is like this—some things are getting harder and some things are getting easier. Sliding downhill can be frightening when we focus on diminishing abilities and it can be fun when we learn how to play on the slide, enjoying who we are like never before.

Spiritual practice catches our attention in an unprecedented way and can be a true source of joy. The people with whom I spoke described a great variety of spiritual practices that are freshly important to them at mid-life. Many spoke about how daily prayer and ritual are wellsprings of joy.

Guru Raj told me about how her daily spiritual practice keeps her connected to her soul.

> For me it's getting up and doing yoga and meditation at 4:30 in the morning—and evening meditation—to keep the channels open. Then it's the million times a day when I allow myself to feel connected to the spirit of life, becoming very present in the moment....I sit, internalize, open, and feel what's really going on. My actions and words have more meaning and depth when I do that.

Morning Tai Chi and meditation allow me to begin each day warmed by God's love. I figure that I can increase my chances of reflecting that love if I first absorb it. Every evening I give thanks for the day's blessings and try to come to terms with those parts of the day's experiences for which I am not so grateful, praying for the grace to learn from them.

Fredelle's daily prayer ritual became richer during the course of having to deal with the limitations and pain of surgery. She began to use a traditional Hebrew prayer book that includes prayers for the beginning and end of the day.

> I compare it to a sandwich. The prayers at the beginning and the end of the day are the container for the filling of what you do during the day. It gives you a sense that God is in control of everything and you don't have to worry too much because nothing is outside the oversight and care of God. I give thanks for the faithfulness of God and I have to

be faithful back to God. The first thing is to thank God for
the intelligence of being able to tell the difference between
day and night.

Fredelle goes on to say that the people with whom she comes into
contact during the day provide her with opportunities to learn more
about God's faithfulness. For her, this becomes a continuous daily process
framed by prayer. Fredelle's experience of diminishing physical strength
enabled her to discover a new source of vitality.

> The experience of being physically weak helped me be
> spiritually stronger because it helped me understand the
> text—the words. When I was stronger I skipped through
> the words and didn't have to really think about them but
> when I was physically weak it took me longer.
> The psalms are a great comfort. "The Lord is My
> Shepherd" is very comforting. The shepherd watches over us
> carefully and leads us away from the danger and into the
> safe place. There is the over-arching, caring, loving God in
> our lives—not a remote figment of our imagination but
> God who is present.

Munir tells me that he not only reads and studies the Koran regularly
but he has also begun to memorize it along with many others around the
world. He already knows about one third of it by heart.

Taking scripture seriously, absorbing it, and reading it carefully
requires time and patience—something that at least some of us may have
in greater supply during the second journey of our lives than we did
during the first. But even for those whose lives remain busy, there may be
a new determination to seize moments of peace. Judy R., for example,
says:

> What gives my life meaning now is being centred in an
> almost Buddhist way, becoming the still point at the centre
> of a turning world. It's those moments of stillness that
> sustain me—preferably in the woods, but even if I can't be
> in the woods, I find a few moments to be still—hiding in

the bathroom or in the back room. If I get moving too fast I lose track of the pulse at the heart of it. Twenty years ago I wasn't aware that there was a pulse. Spirituality then was about noise, about singing and prayer and group activity and all this wild stuff—but now it's just about being still. "Be still, and know that I am God!" has become the crux of it.

I'm not interested in a socially acceptable deity. I've been through many spiritual disciplines over the years. I still do reading from a variety of sources and some journalling but most regularly I try to slow myself down whenever I feel like I'm losing the rhythm of things. I slow down my breathing, focus on the feelings and write the feelings down.

I was once told to write down five feelings in those kinds of moments and whatever is the fifth—the one you come to last—is the one you need to deal with....You can journal on it to stay in touch with the feeling, going with it, working with it, learning from it, and making decisions based on it. Jung believed that God is the central core of everybody and if we get down deep enough we'll find God and I believe that.

Whenever there's a huge question mark, I have to go back to prayer. I just ask God what I'm supposed to do with this: Let go of it? Process it? Or what? And I usually get a clear sense from that. It takes wisdom to know what experiences are worth meditating on and which ones you should just walk away from. I believe in the presence of evil in the world, which is another mid-life revelation and a belief I didn't have twenty years ago. I think there are persons and situations which sap our strength and we shouldn't be meditating on those. We should be walking away from them.

Decades of life experience can help us develop keener spiritual discernment as long as they do not first harden the spiritual arteries by convincing us that we have "been there, done that" and automatically know, for instance, the difference between good and evil.

Nina hones her discerning spirit in very visible ways. She repeats the names of selected deities first thing every morning and takes time to look at their pictures before she leaves the house. She reports that this gives her a sense of power with which to go into the day.

> Every Hindu house has a prayer room and I miss mine when I'm away. Home is the centre of my spiritual life and I'm appreciating that more than ever before. If you came to my house you'd see pictures of gods everywhere.

As a Protestant Christian I was raised to distrust attempts to represent the spirit of God in visible, tangible ways for fear of flirting with idolatry. This meshed easily with my personality type because I was satisfied thinking and speaking about God in words and ideas. But as I am coming into my mid-life senses, enjoying the beauty in what I can see, touch, taste, and smell, I am drawn to liturgies that encompass the full range of ways to experience the divine. I find Nina's practice of filling her home with visible reminders of her spiritual touchstones to be attractive.

I expect that different mid-life personalities will be attracted to different kinds of spiritual practices. Mid-life courage can ensure that we do not get stuck in the spiritual practices we are accustomed to—especially if new ones bring us a greater sense of spirited joy.

Susan told me that it is fidelity to four linked activities that have reshaped her spiritual discipline. The four cornerstones to her days now are reading, writing, walking, and praying. As she moves towards greater integration in mid-life, she finds it essential to involve every part of her being.

> Reading is for my absorbent, intellectual position; writing is the flow where what comes in works itself out; and walking is my equivalent of working in the garden or a Zen discipline of sitting. I find that when I walk whatever I'm thinking about shifts and moves. It's my focused, meditative time when I can hear what I need to hear....The pulse of the heart and the pulse of the mind and rhythm of legs and hands are all working in concert and I feel that kind of aliveness—that real awareness that's central. From that

grows the kind of quickening of gratitude that grows into
prayer. It cheers me up when I learn that someone in
twelfth-century France was doing this and that there is a
Zen walking meditation. What I do isn't glamorous—it's
just very simple, rudimentary, and crucial to my well-being.

As a member of the post-war generation known as baby boomers, I
realize that we are susceptible to thinking of ourselves as the first
generation to deal with mid-life just as we thought we were the first
generation to have children! Our large numbers have led to self-
centredness. But Susan reminds us that many of the spiritual practices
that appeal to us are really quite ancient.

Making a pilgrimage to a holy, healing place is another age-old
practice that many seem to be rediscovering. Ralph frequently goes on
pilgrimage to the Indian community of Gobind Sadam and visits with
Baba Virsa Singh ji. He has learned how to speak Punjabi, which indi-
cates his commitment to the place and the community. Whenever he is
called to show up for an important event there, he leaves his insurance
business in the United States and simply goes.

> Gobind Sadan is 240 acres of peace. I consider it the pre-
> eminent spiritual institution in the world and just try to live
> up to its standards. It is pure spiritual peace...it's like you
> walk into the spiritual dimension. With practice, I'm getting
> better at walking in and out.

Earlier in these pages both Mary and Paul spoke about the importance
of finding a community—a circle of people—with whom they could
meet regularly and experience complete safety and support while sharing
their mid-life journey. Beth is typical, I think, of many mid-lifers who
yearn for this kind of community to support their mid-life spiritual
development.

> One outlet I'm seriously missing is the chance to talk
> about spiritual issues in my life. That outlet does not exist for
> me and I keep wondering when it's going to exist for me or
> thinking maybe it will be there if I get cancer or something.

Perhaps then I'll suddenly have a group to talk to—but where is that community under normal circumstances? If one of my neighbours who I consider a good friend knocked on my door and invited me to go to any kind of meaningful worship service, I'd likely go. I don't think I'm vulnerable to anything but there's a real gap and hunger that I have no idea how to satisfy. If it came my way, I'd grab at it.

There is a challenge to religious communities in what Beth says, and no reason why we cannot create mid-life circles of spiritual support with the benefit of her advice. She suggests that the religious community should not assume that the secular world does not offer resources for spiritual nourishment. She also suggests that whatever we do in this regard should not add to what we may already experience as a great burden of obligation.

Reading literature, or watching a TV show or movie in which the issues of mortality and life and meaning are explored, or having good conversations with friends, or listening to good music, or watching a good play are sources of spiritual nourishment. I'm irritated that most of my life I've sought to find all this in one place whereas all of a sudden, by golly, I can find it in other places—and people in other places are just as good or kind or bad or whatever as they are in the church.

I joined a garden club where I pay seven dollars a year and I don't have to do anything—I can be as involved as I want to be and if I don't go it's okay. But I had to convince myself that I could do that without exploiting it—that I didn't have to give back more. And after three years, one day they asked me to design a window box so I did it and won first prize. I was so pleased to do it because they never asked anything else of me. The purpose of the group wasn't to ask things of me. I thought, "what a neat concept!" to have 150 people come out once a month and they don't need a lot of money or to sign in blood but a common bond brings us together.

Beth's words brought me back to thinking about the difference between bondage and responsibility that we explored in chapter six. We will no longer be bound by spiritual practices that do not nourish us in mid-life but we can find new and renewed ways to make responsible action part of our spiritual discipline.

Religious communities frequently provide us with a wonderful network through which to become involved in constructive action for justice and peace. As Vice-Chair of the Canadian Jewish Congress Ontario region, Esta says: "When you're Jewish, you always have a meeting to go to." Socially active Christians and others would say the same! And some of us only come to a dawning of global awareness once we're mid-lifers. Angelos told me about how he has matured in his thinking about others in the world.

> I had the opportunity to go to Lagos, Nigeria, for a few weeks with my job. I saw people who were so impoverished—living on the street, bathing in water from sewers—and they were so happy. They were living life to the fullest and that had an impact on me. These people have nothing and they're happy with their lives. That's when I shifted my thinking too. When I was younger I wanted a Cadillac and the fanciest suit and now I don't care. We're better off than 90 percent of the people on this earth so let's be happy. I'm more responsive to international appeals now.

I saw a deep sense of joy shining through Angelos' words and the reasons for that joy are, I think, explained by something Hugh said to me.

> I saw a survey in which people over ninety-five were asked what they would do differently if they had it to do again and the three big things were reflect more, risk more, and invest more—and when they said invest more they meant in relationships. I remember in my thirties, I was so darned anxious about everything—about money, status, security, and how people saw me. I wanted to be seen, and I worked so hard and thought I was doing such good work. I'd see clients day and night. I wouldn't do that anymore and

if I had to do it again, I wouldn't do it—I'd invest
differently.

My body is teaching me to be selective about the kinds
of stress I put myself in when given the choice. I'm very
selective about who I spend time with now too. I choose to
be with people of substance and those who are not negative.

Hugh demonstrates once again that we can choose not to be bound
but to be joyfully liberated.

The wonder of what we can learn from attending to our dreams is yet
another dimension to mid-life spiritual practice. I remember interviewing
Morton Kelsey who has written several books on the relationship
between dreams and religion. He told me about how God breaks into
our lives through dreams and that because dreams are creative, they are
divine. Volumes have been written about what we can learn from our
dreams and Flora gave me one mid-life example.

I have found understanding my dreams to be important
to my mid-life passage as I to try to glean wisdom. I work
with the images in my dreams and enter dialogue with them
and they show me what is going on inside which I may be
reluctant to see. For example, my dreams had many baby
and child images and I came to understand that they
represented the beginning of a new life in me, with the
integration of the conscious and unconscious, the two sides
of myself coming together. And I believe that's what mid-life
is—it's a coming home to oneself, to who we really are,
dropping off masks and roles—even before ourselves—
which is where it has to happen first. It's like being the
velveteen rabbit—becoming real.

Flora's reference to Margery Williams' book, *The Velveteen Rabbit*,
reminds me of the importance of knowing that we are loved. Her words
also suggest that we may finally be able to love ourselves at mid-life.
Feeling loved and loving in response is, I believe, the source of greatest joy
for the mid-life soul.

The conversations shared in the pages of this book reinforce the damental importance of this acceptance of ourselves and others, and of appreciating differences as we allow for our own souls and others' to mature gracefully.

Munir explained to me his belief that God has made us different in order to find the incentive to excel and to appreciate, complement, and meet one another's needs.

Joan Didion is right when she says that it is impossible to ever get to the point of seeing a clearly marked open road to the years ahead but the companionship of one another can open our souls to receive the guidance we yearn for. That's certainly how these interviews have affected me, and it is why I continue to enjoy being with other mid-lifers on retreat. Our mid-life retreats (at Naramata and Five Oaks Centre) enable people to become companions to one another and to learn how to embrace the emerging, new mid-life dimensions of themselves. We are able to support one another in a community that celebrates diversity.

We do this through a mixture of writing, telling, and listening to our life stories; of offering and receiving open questions to help us discern our concerns and our next steps; of writing ourselves into future scenarios and proclaiming our births into the second journey. Journal writing, singing, discussion, silence, and prayer all have their place. These provide the essential elements to help us accompany one another as mid-life souls.

In short, we open our souls and ready ourselves to receive guidance to meet radically new challenges in our spiritual journeys. We discover yet again that we are not alone—that we are deeply loved and capable of loving more deeply. We are invited to come closer than ever before to the loving Source of our mid-life crisis and joy.

I believe that God intends us to enjoy life's adventure including the dangerous, exciting, confusing, and reassuring twists and turns of mid-life. If it feels like you are sliding, my advice is to share the experience and enjoy the ride!

# Notes

page 10. Elliot Jaques' work is also cited in Gail Sheehy's *Passages: Predictable Crises of Adult Life* (Toronto: Bantam, 1977©1976).

page 12. Daniel Levinson is a psychologist who has written extensively on developmental theories.

page 15. Erik Erikson, *The Life Cycle Completed* (New York: Norton, 1963); Allan Chinen, *Once upon a Midlife: Classic Stories and Mythic Tales to Illuminate the Middle Years* (New York: Jeremy P. Tarcher/Putnam, 1992). p. 27.

page 31. Erma Bombeck, *The Standard-Times*, New Bedford, Mass., May 1977.

page 48. Ted Loder, *Guerrillas of Grace* (Philadelphia: Innisfree Press Inc., 1984) pp. 48–49.

page 50. Carl G. Jung, *Psychological Types* (Princeton NJ: Princeton University Press, 1971).

page 52. Eleanor S. Corlett and Nancy B. Millner, *Navigating Midlife: Using Typology as a Guide* (Palo Alto CA: CPP Books, 1993).

page 59. Carlita Figueroa-Faxton, *Getting the Love That You Need: A Guide to Understanding Each Other & Learning How to Love*, edited by Donna Rey and Megun Wills (New York: Carlita Faxton, n.d.).

page 102. Frederick Buechner, *Wishful Thinking: A Seeker's ABC* (San Francisco: HarperSanFrancisco, 1993) p. 95.

page 103. Paul Tillich is a well-known theologian whose books include *The Courage to Be*.

page 104. Bible quote is a paraphrase of Psalm 20:4. Joseph Campbell was a pre-eminent scholar, writer, and teacher known for his authoritative work on mythology.

page 109–110. A. Powell Davies, *Life Prayers: from around the World: 365 Prayers, Blessings, and Affirmations to Celebrate the Human Journey*, edited by Elizabeth Roberts and Elias Amidon (New York: Harper Collins, 1996) p. 96.

page 118. Psalm 46:10.

page 123. Morton Kelsey has written extensively on Christianity, healing, and dreams. His books include *Dreams—A Way to Listen to God* (Mahwah, NJ: Paulist Press, 1978). Margery Williams, *The Velveteen Rabbit*, illustrated by William Nicholson (New York: Doubleday & Co.)

# Resources Consulted

Brehony, Kathleen A. *Awakening at Midlife* New York: Riverhead Books, 1996

Brennan, Anne and Janice Brewi. *Mid-Life Directions: Praying and Playing Sources of New Dynamism* Mahwah, NJ: Paulist Press, 1985

Carroll, L. Patrick, S.J. and Katherine Marie Dyckman S.N.J.M. *Chaos or Creation: Spirituality in Mid-Life*, Mahwah, NJ: Paulist Press, 1986

Chinen, Allan B., M.D. *Once Upon a Midlife: Classic Stories and Mythic Tales to Illuminate the Middle Years* New York: Jeremy P. Tarcher/Putnam, 1992

Corlett, Eleanor S. and Nancy B. Millner. *Navigating Midlife: Using Typology as a Guide* Palo Alto, CA: CPP Books, 1993

Fowler, Jim and Sam Keen. *Life Maps: Conversations on the Journey of Faith* Nashville: Word Publishing, 1978

Gerzon, Mark. *Listening to Midlife: Turning Your Crisis into a Quest* Boston, MA: Shambhala, 1996

Harris, Maria. *Jubilee Time* New York: Bantam Books, 1995

Levinson, Daniel J. *The Seasons of a Man's Life* New York: Knopf, 1978

———. *The Seasons of a Woman's Life* New York: Ballantine Books, 1996

Olsen, Richard P. *Midlife Journeys* Cleveland: The Pilgrim Press, 1996

Rupp, Joyce. *Dear Heart, Come Home: The Path of Midlife Spirituality* New York: The Crossroad Publishing Company, 1996

# Credits

page 1.   Reprinted with the permission of Simon & Shuster from After Henry by Joan Didion. Copyright ©1992 by Joan Didion.

page 5.   From **Larry's Party by Carol Shields**. Copyright © 1997. Reprinted by permission of Random House of Canada Limited. English language, Canadian rights only. From *LARRY'S PARTY* by Carol Shields, copyright © 1997 by Carol Shields. Used by permission of Viking Penguin, a division of Penguin Putnam Inc.

page 25.  From **Larry's Party by Carol Shields**. Copyright © 1997. Reprinted by permission of Random House of Canada Limited. English language, Canadian rights only. From *LARRY'S PARTY* by Carol Shields, copyright © 1997 by Carol Shields. Used by permission of Viking Penguin, a division of Penguin Putnam Inc.

page 44.  Quotation from *Guerrillas of Grace* by Ted Loder, ©1984, reprinted by permission of Innisfree Press, Inc.

page 45.  Alberto Manguel, from *The Globe and Mail*, 13 Feb. 1999, D16.

page 63.  From **A Certain Justice by P.D. James**. Copyright ©1998. Reprinted by permission of Alfred A. Knopf Canada. English language, Canadian rights only; US rights granted by Alfred A. Knopf a Division of Random House Inc.

page 79.  From *Memory Lane* by Laurence Gough © 1997. Used by permission, McClelland & Stewart, Inc. *The Canadian Publishers*.

page 97.  From MEMOIRS OF A GEISHA by Arthur Golden with permission of Alfred A. Knopf a Division of Random House Inc.